About the Author

Geneviève Crabe

Geneviève Crabe has been working in the high-tech industry since 1978 and is the author of *Macintosh Graphic Techniques for Multimedia*. A lifelong crafter, she recently took up decorative painting, and is now a certified instructor for Donna Dewberry's One Stroke™ technique. She combined her love of crafts and knowledge of the Internet to create this book and the companion Web site, **http://www.craftersinternet.com/**.

Dedication

I dedicate this book to all my online friends. Thanks for all the help, support, and encouragement.

Acknowledgments

This book has greatly benefited from many outstanding contributions. I want to thank Melinda Barnes for all the painting links, Susan Brandt for the copyright article, Ronit Florence for the cross-stitch information, Heather Fox for a great interview on craftideas.com, Marie Gemmil for information on the Memory Box Project, Tera Leigh for her article on creativity, Shelley McCoy and Beth Koskie for their thoughts on crafting for charity, Sharon Saunders for her wonderful wisdom, Anne Strebe for a terrific interview about ToleFriends, Phyllis Tilford for her ideas on Web sites and e-commerce, Jennifer and Matt Turpin, auctioneers extraordinaire, and all my online friends from these discussion lists: the Toronto OneStroke certification group, OneStroke Painting, the Memory Box Program, ToleFriends, and the OSCI list.

Special thanks to my agent, Carole McClendon from Waterside Productions, for understanding what this book meant to me. And many thanks to the wonderful people at Muska & Lipman, including Andy Shafran, Hope Stephan, Allen Wyatt, Rodney Wilson, Mark Garvey, Sherri Osborn, and Sherri Schwartz.

Contents

10—Finding Supplies 133

Section V: Selling and Marketing Online

11—What to Sell Online 157

12—How to Sell Online 171

13—Creating Your Web Site 187

Introduction

*"Use what talent you possess: the woods would be very silent
if no birds sang except those that sang best."*

—Henry Van Dyke

When I was young, I taught myself needlepoint and crochet, and I quite happily pursued these crafts on my own for many years. A couple of years ago, I took up decorative painting as a new hobby. By that time, I had already been using the Internet for many years, so it was a natural thing for me to start looking for craft information online. With this book, I want to share some of what I have discovered by providing a "travel guide" to help you find your way on the Internet.

With millions of people, and hundreds of thousands of Web sites, the Internet can be overwhelming, especially if you're just getting started. I hope this book will take some of the mystery out of it for you and help you to feel more comfortable online.

Sometimes people get hung up on the technology aspect of the Internet. For me, the Internet is all about connections—connecting with information and products, yes, but most of all, connecting with people. I have made many friends all over the world during my online travels, and I look forward to sharing some of those experiences with you.

Who Can Use This Book?

If you enjoy doing any kind of craft, from needlework to decorative painting, this book is for you. You will find something of interest whether you are a hobbyist or a business crafter, a beginner or a seasoned crafter.

I will assume that you already have access to the Internet and that, if I say "e-mail" or "Web site," you know what I am talking about. I will explain more advanced topics in detail. If I were to compare this to a craft like crochet, I would assume you already know the very basic stuff like how to make a chain stitch but not much else.

This Book is Organized

will provide you with an introduction to a whole series of topics. Entire books have en about the topics I cover in each chapter, and what I hope to accomplish is for you to become acquainted with all these topics, understand the terminology, and perhaps go on to learn more on your own.

Section One: The Internet covers the basics of e-mail and the World Wide Web. When you get done with this section, you will have a much firmer grip on how to use e-mail and navigate the Web.

In **Section Two: Researching Online**, we move on to learning about search engines, directories, and ways of finding information. You'll also find out how to spark your creativity and what you need to know about copyright and licensing issues. When you get done with this section, you will be better equipped to find what you are looking for.

The Internet is a wonderful tool for connecting with people who have common interests. **Section Three: Connecting Online** will introduce you to online communities, discussion lists, and crafting for charity projects. Joining discussion lists will open your horizons by giving you the opportunity to interact with people all over the world.

Section Four: Buying Online will cover what you need to know about online shopping, including safe shopping tips and how to find suppliers. If you have never shopped online before, the information in this chapter will make you feel more confident; you will know what to look for to make sure your information is secure.

The theme of **Section Five: Selling and Marketing Online** is how you can use the Internet to enhance your craft business. The topics include market research, how to sell online, creating your own Web site, and marketing. If you are so inclined, this information will get you started on the road to electronic commerce.

The **Web site** for this book contains a collection of Web links that I have visited over the past few months. You will find links related to every chapter and section in the book.

If you use the Web, you know that it's a very fluid place where things change all the time. People find great freedom in the fact that they can update or change their Web sites quickly and often. As a result, you may find that the screen shots in the book are not identical to what you will see when you visit the sites. Many sites change some of the elements on their main page weekly, or even daily. So use the screen shots as a guide, but don't expect a totally identical look when you visit the sites.

Furthermore, some of the sites I mention in the book may have disappeared altogether, and there will be new sites out there that didn't exist when I wrote the book. Again, this is the nature of the Internet. This is why, instead of simply telling you *where* to find things, I explain *how* to find things—so that you will have the tools you need to find whatever you are looking for.

I have created a companion Web site for the book at **http://www.craftersinternet.com/**. This site will contain some updates and additions to the book, the comprehensive set of Web links mentioned in this book, a discussion list, and a few additional goodies.

I hope you'll come and visit.

Section I
The Internet

"I may not have gone where I intended to go,
but I think I have ended up where I intended to be."

—Douglas Adams

1

E-Mail

Electronic mail, more commonly called e-mail, consists of sending a message from one computer to another over the Internet. This usually happens very quickly, sometimes in a few minutes, and except for what it costs you to connect to the Internet in the first place, it's essentially free. You can send a message to anyone who has an e-mail account, anywhere in the world, almost instantly. Every day more people get on the Internet, and so more people become reachable by e-mail.

In its simplest form, when you send an e-mail message, you are sending a text file; additionally, you can send images, documents created in a word processor, or other types of files. In this chapter, you'll learn how to send images and other files in your e-mail messages and how to organize your e-mail.

E-Mail Accounts

I assume that you already have some form of Internet access, including an e-mail account. If you don't have an e-mail account set up, consult your Internet Service provider for instructions on how to do this. There are also Web-based e-mail accounts, many of which are provided at no charge. I will describe these in Chapter 2.

An e-mail account usually comes with whatever Internet service you subscribe to. The information you received when you signed up should include your e-mail address, which looks something like this:

name@company.com

The part before the @ is your user name, which can be your name, nickname, or some other word you choose when you set up your Internet account. The part after the @ is known as a "domain" name, which represents your Internet service provider (ISP). For example, if you use America Online, your e-mail address would be name@aol.com, or, if you use the cable-based @Home service, it would be name@home.com.

Your e-mail address is unique on the Internet, which means that no two people can have the same e-mail address, so anyone can send e-mail to that address to reach you. Unlike your street address, though, it's possible for you to have more than one e-mail address; think of it like a post office box, where you can have more than one to use for different purposes.

Sending and Receiving E-Mail

There are several different software programs you can use to send and receive e-mail; I use Microsoft Outlook Express version 5 for Macintosh (see Figure 1.1), and this is what I used for the screen shots you will see in this section. If you use a different program, you will find that most of the functions and commands will be similar in your program, although your program may look different.

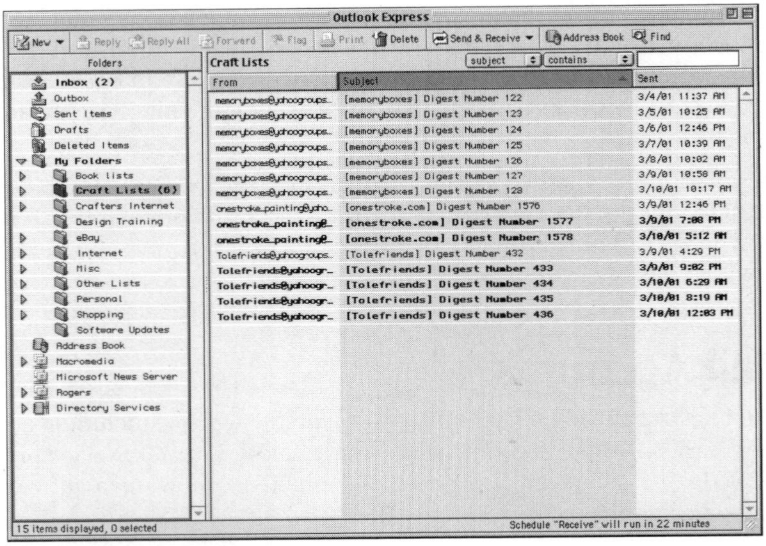

Figure 1.1

The main window of Microsoft's Outlook Express for Macintosh.

NOTE

Please remember that, throughout this chapter, I have been using Microsoft Outlook Express for Macintosh. The features I describe are general ones that are available in most e-mail programs, although the way they are used may be different. If you use a different program, you may have to consult your manual or Help files to find out how to use the functions I describe.

Composing and Sending a Message

To create a message in Outlook Express, choose the **New Mail Message** command from the **File** menu; there should be a similar command in any e-mail program. When you compose a message, there are several fields for you to fill in (see Figure 1.2).

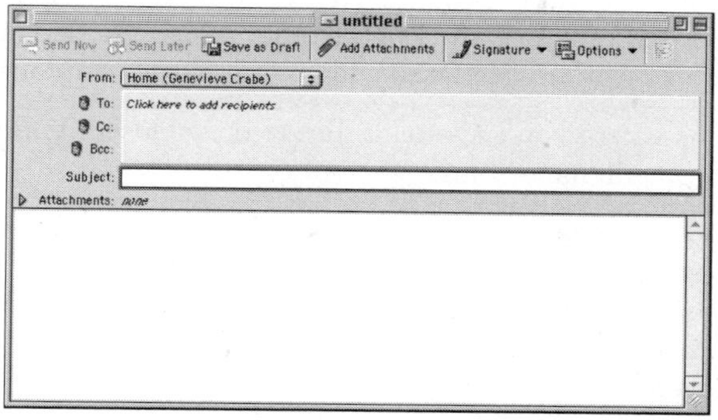

Figure 1.2
Preparing to compose a new message.

Table 1.1. shows the fields you need for a basic message:

Table 1.1
Basic e-mail message fields

To	This is where you insert the e-mail addresses of your message's main recipients. Check the manual or the Help files for your e-mail software to see how to enter multiple addresses.
Subject	This is a short description of your message that the recipient will be able to see before opening the message.
Content	This is where you type the text of your message.

The To field is mandatory. Some e-mail programs will force you to put something in the Subject and Content fields, while others will happily let you send a message with no subject and no content. Your message can also contain some optional fields, shown in Table 1.2, that you might use on occasion.

Table 1.2

Additional e-mail message fields

Cc	This is the copy-to field, for the e-mail addresses of people who are secondary recipients of the message.
Bcc	This is the blind-copy field. These people will receive the message, but their names will not be shown to the other recipients. This is useful if you are sending out a newsletter to a large number of recipients.
Attachments	This is where you can attach files to be enclosed with your message, for example, digital photos.
From	You don't usually change the From field—it contains your own e-mail address and is automatically filled in. But if you have several e-mail accounts that you use for different purposes, you can have a choice of which e-mail address you want to appear in the From field. Keep in mind that this is the address that replies will be sent to.

For example, here is a message I might send to a friend. Notice that all the standard fields are in this sample message: To, Subject, and Content (or body).

To: kirsten@someinternetprovider.com
Subject: Painting on fabric

Hi Kirsten,
I was wondering if you can help me out. What brand of paint do
you use for painting on t-shirts? Do you use fabric medium? What about brushes?

Thanks,
Geneviève

In addition to the standard fields, most e-mail programs allow you to define one or more signatures. These usually contain your name, e-mail address, and a few more lines of text depending on the context, for example, your title, the address of your Web site, or a favorite quote. Some e-mail programs allow you to define several signatures, so that you can have one suitable for any circumstance. To send a message, you fill in the appropriate fields and click **Send**. The software takes care of the rest.

To make it easier for you to remember the e-mail addresses of your friends and acquaintances, e-mail programs include an "electronic" address book. It allows you to store the names and e-mail addresses of people you often communicate with and call them up easily when you compose a message.

Receiving a Message

If you are connected to the Internet when you open your e-mail program, the program may automatically check for new mail. If not, there should be a menu item or button labeled something like **Get Mail** to get your mail.

In Figure 1.1, you can see on the left a list of "folders" that contain messages. When you receive a message, it usually resides in a special folder called the Inbox. In most e-mail programs, the messages in your Inbox appear as a list in the right-hand pane showing the sender, subject, and the date and time. You can open a message by double-clicking it in the list. In Figure 1.1, you can see that some of the messages are bold; these are the messages I haven't read yet. Because they are bold, I can easily see which messages are new. The number in parentheses next to the Inbox on the left also tells me I have unread messages (in this case, two).

Table 1.3 lists some standard things you can do with a message you have received besides reading it:

Table 1.3
What you can do with a message

Reply	Clicking the **Reply** button automatically creates a new message addressed to the originator of the message you are replying to.
Forward	Clicking the **Forward** button creates a copy of the message you received, ready for you to send on to someone else.
Print	The **Print** button allows you to print the messages you have received.
Delete	Once you no longer need the message, clicking on the Delete button discards it. In some e-mail programs, the message is deleted immediately; in others, it is moved to a special folder called "Trash" or "Deleted Items," which either empties itself periodically or must be emptied manually.

Organizing Your Messages

When you start receiving a lot of e-mail, it is necessary for you to find ways to keep the messages organized. You can create folders to do this. Also, some e-mail programs allow you to automate some of this organization. The next couple of sections examine some of the ways in which you can organize your e-mail.

Folders

In e-mail programs like Outlook Express, you can create folders to organize your messages. You can store messages you have received and copies of messages you have sent.

In Figure 1.3, you can see the folders I have created under My Folders. In Outlook Express, you create folders using the **New Folder** command in the **File** menu. Each folder represents a category, just like you might use file folders to organize paper mail. Electronic folders have the added advantage that you can create folders within folders; this helps to keep things tidy, especially if you receive a lot of e-mail.

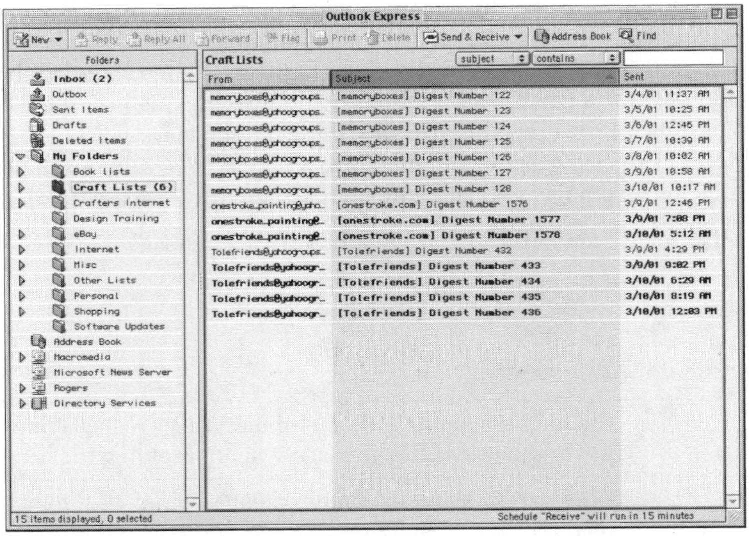

Figure 1.3
Creating folders
helps you organize
your e-mail.

In my case, I have a folder where I keep e-mails from crafting mailing lists and one for book-related lists. I also have one for messages related to my online shopping, one for personal messages, and so on. Once you have created the folders, you can move messages into them by dragging them from the right-hand side to the folder name on the left.

Now that you have all your e-mail nicely organized, there are several features you can use to find messages. When you are looking at the contents of a folder, you can choose how the messages are listed. Look at the headings above the list of messages in Figure 1.3—you see how the **Subject** heading is darker? This is because the messages are sorted by Subject. If I click the **Sent** heading, the messages will be sorted by the time they were sent (see Figure 1.4).

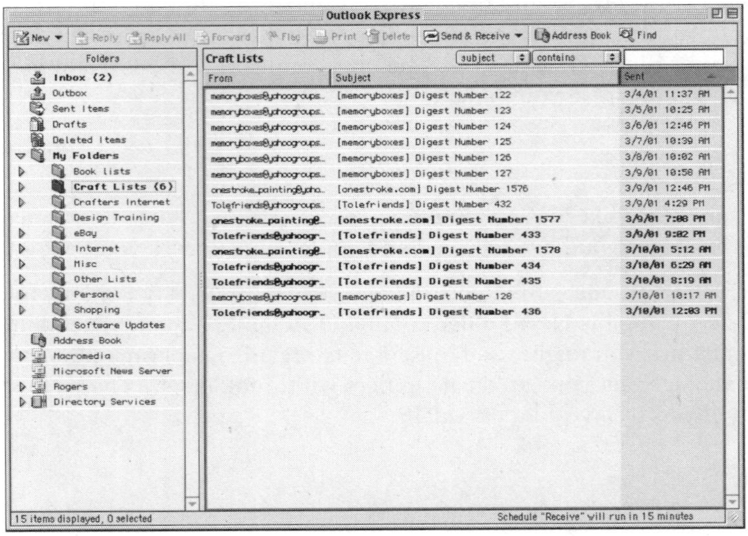

Figure 1.4
A message list sorted
by date and time sent
(oldest first).

Note that the list is displayed in chronological order. If I click the **Sent** heading a second time, the order is reversed (see Figure 1.5) and the list is displayed in reverse chronological order. You can click any of the headings to change how the list is sorted.

Figure 1.5
The same list sorted by date and time sent (newest first).

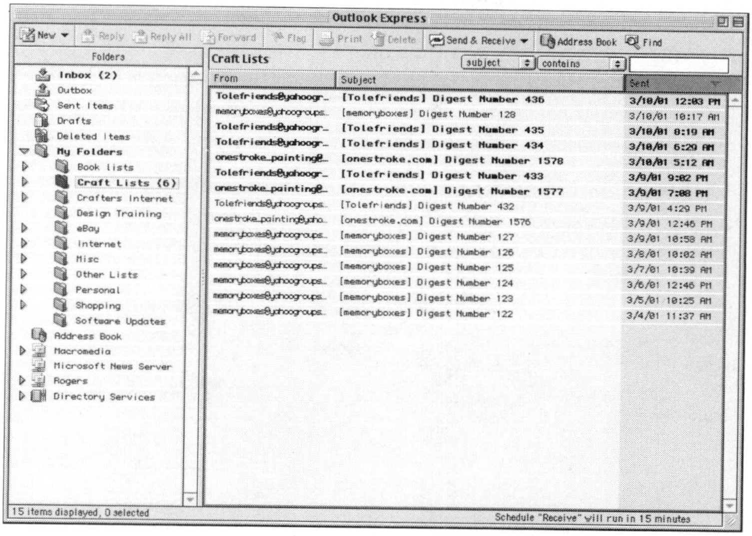

You can also use the **Find** feature (see Figure 1.6), which is in the **Edit** menu in Outlook Express, to locate specific messages. You can search for all the messages from a particular person by searching the To field or search for messages on a certain topic by searching the Subject.

For example, say I wanted to find all the messages from Jane Smith, and I know that they are filed in various folders. I would enter "Jane Smith" in the text field in the Find window. I would check the **From** box because that is where I want to look for the name, and I would click **All Folders** under Location so that all folders are searched. The results will appear in a separate window, listing all the messages from Jane Smith.

Figure 1.6
The Find window in Outlook Express.

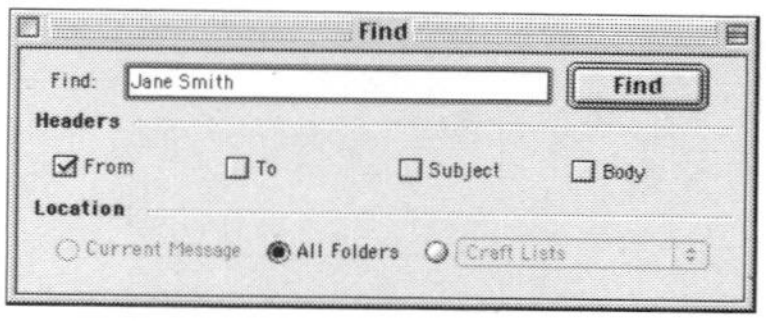

Filters

Many e-mail programs allow you to create filters for your incoming mail, directing certain messages to be immediately stored in specific folders. In Outlook Express, you do this by setting up rules, using the **Rules** command in the **Tools** menu.

Here is an example. One of the mailing lists I subscribe to is Donna Dewberry's One Stroke Painting mailing list. I thought it would be nice if the messages from this list (and others) were put directly into their own folders as soon as they arrive instead of all showing up in the Inbox. This is especially useful since I subscribe to many mailing lists on a variety of topics.

First, I created a folder called "Craft Lists" for all my craft-related mailing lists. Then, I set up the rule shown in Figure 1.7 so that all the messages coming from the One Stroke list are automatically put in my Craft Lists folder instead of the Inbox.

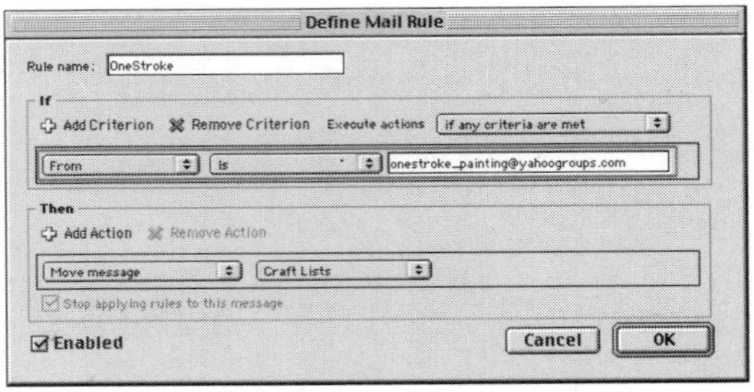

Figure 1.7
The Define Mail Rule window allows you to direct incoming e-mail messages to a specific folder.

The first part of the rule tells the software what to look for—in this case, look for a message from onestroke_painting@yahoogroups.com, which is the e-mail address of the list. The second part tells the software what to do—in this case, move the message to the folder called Craft Lists.

Figure 1.8 shows another example. In this case, if the Subject of the message contains the word "Urgent," the computer will play a sound and print the message. The **Enabled** checkbox means that this rule is active. You can use this checkbox to temporarily turn off a rule without having to delete it.

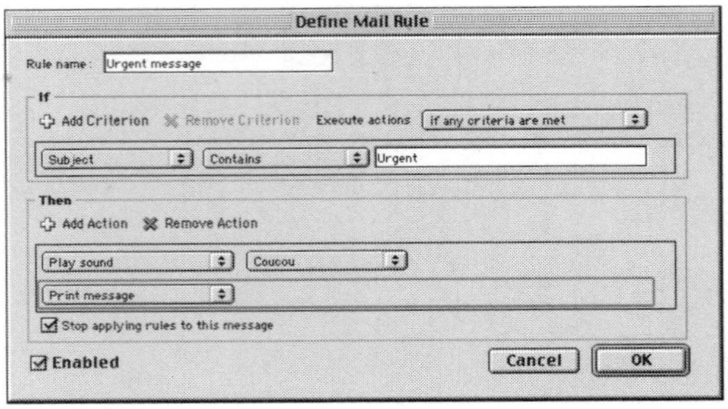

Figure 1.8
The Define Mail Rule can also be used to tell your e-mail program how to handle certain kinds of messages.

The Rules feature is very powerful. The more e-mail you receive, the more you can use the rules to help you manage the messages.

http://www.muskalipman.com

Attachments

You can attach files to the e-mail messages you send. For example, say you want to show a picture of a sweater you knitted to an online friend. You have several options for getting a picture of the item into the computer:

▶ You can take a photograph of the sweater, then once the photograph is developed, you can use a scanner to scan the picture into your computer.

▶ If the item is flat, like a greeting card, you can scan the item itself into the computer.

▶ If you have a digital camera, you can take a picture and transfer the image directly from the camera to the computer.

▶ If you don't have a scanner or a digital camera, you can take a picture with a regular camera and then, when you get the film developed, ask for a photo CD. You will get a CD containing all your pictures in digital format, and you can copy the pictures to your computer.

If you are sending a photograph, you should use a format called JPEG (or JPG). This is a format that saves a photograph in good quality, but the file size is fairly small, which is important for sending files by e-mail.

Once you have the picture in the computer, it's a simple thing to attach it to a message. In Outlook Express, you click the **Add Attachments** button (see Figure 1.2) to open a window where you can browse through your hard disk and find the file.

If you receive e-mail messages with attached images, many e-mail programs will display the image right in the content field. To show this, I sent a message to myself containing a picture of a memory box I painted. Figure 1.9 shows the message as I received it. If your e-mail program doesn't do this, check your manual or Help files to see how to display image attachments.

Figure 1.9
An e-mail message
displaying the
attached image.

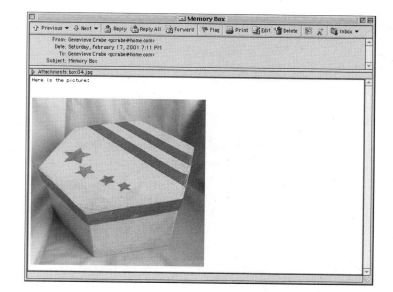

It is possible to send other kinds of files as attachments in an e-mail message, such as documents, spreadsheets, and even applications. The same mechanism is used to attach any type of file; in Outlook Express, use the **Add Attachments** button.

Just as you may send a message that contains attachments, you might also receive one that has an attachment. In the Inbox (see Figure 1.1), you can tell that a message contains an attachment by the paperclip icon. When a message contains an attachment, there is an indication in the message window. In Figure 1.10, you can see the Attachment below the Subject. In this case, the attachment is a Microsoft Word document called Cross-Stitch Tips.doc.

Figure 1.10
This e-mail message
has an attachment.

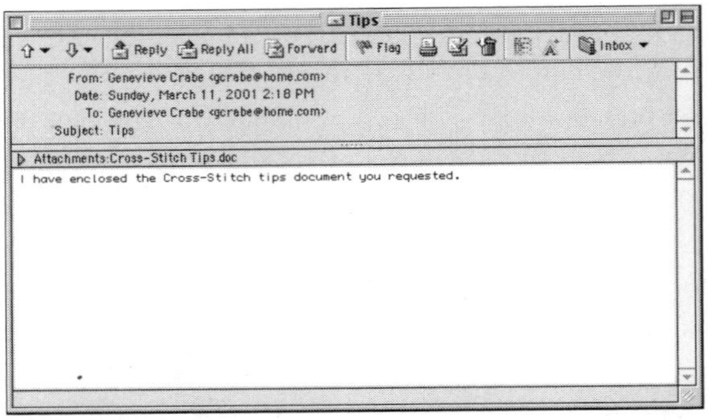

If you click the triangle next to the word Attachment, you get more information, as shown in Figure 1.11. You can choose to open the attachment, delete it, or save it to your hard disk. If you choose the **Save** option, make sure you remember where you saved it so you can find it again later.

Figure 1.11
Click on the Attachment
area to see more
information about the
file you have received
and to access options
for dealing with it.

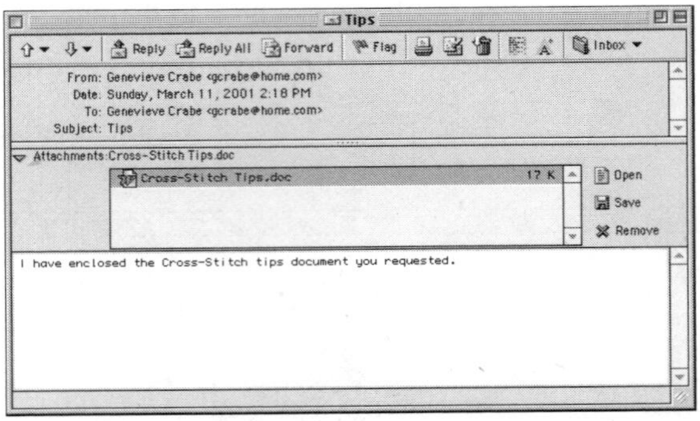

When you save an attachment, navigate to the folder where you want to save the document and click **Save**. Later you can find the document again (see Figure 1.12) and double-click the icon to open it.

Figure 1.12
The saved attachments show their filenames and file types.

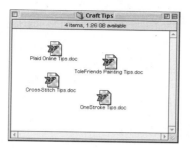

CAUTION

When receiving a message with an attachment other than a picture, you have to be careful, because certain kinds of attachments can contain viruses. The best way to protect yourself is to have virus protection software on your computer and make sure the virus definitions are kept up to date.

Two Web sites you can use to keep up with information on viruses are:

McAfee **http://www.mcafee.com/**

Symantec Anti-Virus Center **http://www.symantec.com/avcenter**

Viruses can even masquerade as messages that look like they are coming from someone you know. You should never open an attachment unless you know what it is and whom it's from; if you're not sure, contact the sender first. For Windows users, be especially suspicious of attachment with extensions .exe and .vbs.

2
The Web

The World Wide Web (also referred to as WWW) is a global collection of hundreds of millions of interconnected electronic "pages" of information covering just about every topic you can think of. These pages usually contain text and images, and some also include animation, sound, or video. In this chapter, you will learn how to use a program called a Web browser to access this information via the Internet.

A collection of Web pages is called a Web site. There are Web sites that belong to individuals and some that belong to corporations. Just about anyone with Internet access can create a Web site. For us crafters, the Web contains a wealth of information, from individual crafters who share tips and techniques to crafting magazines that offer free project sheets to sites where you can shop for craft supplies.

Your Web Browser

A browser (see Figure 2.1) is a program that you use to visit Web sites on the Internet. Web pages are displayed in the browser window, and "links" are used to go to other pages. Links are words and graphics that you click to navigate through the Web. These will be explained in more detailed below.

There are two major Web browsers: Netscape Navigator (which I will refer to simply as Netscape) and Microsoft Internet Explorer (referred to as IE). Their basic functions are similar, at least to the extent that I will be covering them in this book. Of course, you also need to have Internet access from an Internet service provider (ISP).

In this chapter, I will explain some of the differences between the browsers, using Netscape version 4.7 and IE version 5.0 on a Macintosh computer; in the rest of the book, the screen shots were made with IE, but whether you are using Windows instead of Macintosh, or Netscape instead of IE, things should not look too different inside the browser window.

Figure 2.1
The Internet Explorer
Web browser showing
a Web page in the
main window and its
description at the top
of the screen.

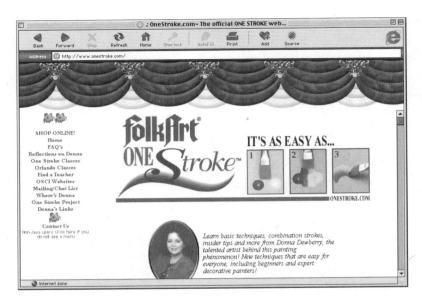

TIP

There are a few differences in terminology between Netscape and IE that you
should be aware of:

Netscape	Internet Explorer
Bookmarks	Favorites
Location bar	Address Bar
Reload	Refresh
Personal Toolbar	Favorites Bar

Netscape

Figure 2.2 shows Netscape Navigator, which is part of the Netscape Communicator package. The
Navigation toolbar contains some of the most-often used menu commands (those same
commands are also in the menus). The Location toolbar contains the URL or address of the Web
page currently displayed; I'll explain more about URLs (Uniform Resource Locators) later in this
chapter. For now, think of a URL as the address of a Web page. The Status bar shows various bits
of information about what is happening on the Web page.

Figure 2.2
The Netscape Web browser showing the same Web page in the main window and its description at the top of the page.

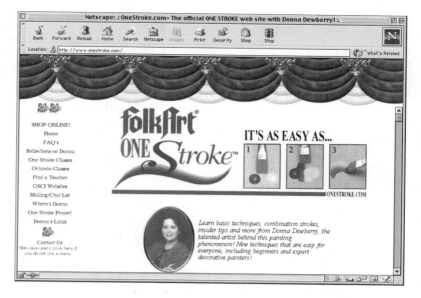

The Navigation toolbar (see Figure 2.3) contains buttons for common functions. Here are the ones most commonly used:

Table 2.1
Navigation Buttons

Back	Go back to the previous page. You'll find yourself using this one all the time; it's a way to backtrack when you've taken a wrong turn or when you want to retrace your steps. This command is also found in the Go menu.
Forward	Go to the page you were on when you clicked the back button. This command is also found in the Go menu.
Reload	Reload (or Refresh in IE) the current page, to display the current version of the page. This command is also found in the View menu.
Home	Go to the Home page, which you have defined in Preferences or Settings. This is the first page that comes up when you launch the browser. This command is also found in the View menu.
Print	Print the current page. Sometimes, the page contains advertisements and other extraneous bits of information that will also appear in your printout. On some pages, you will find a link labeled Print-friendly version; clicking this link will take you to a page with the same content, but without the extra stuff. This command is also found in the File menu.
Stop	Stop loading the current page; this is useful when you change your mind and you don't want to wait for the whole page to load. This command is also found in the View menu.

Figure 2.3
The Netscape
navigation toolbar.

Internet Explorer

Figure 2.4 shows Microsoft Internet Explorer. The Button bar contains some of the most-often-used commands (those same commands are also in the menus). The Address bar contains the URL or address of the Web page currently displayed. The Status bar shows various bits of information about what is happening on the Web page.

Figure 2.4
The Internet Explorer
Web browser

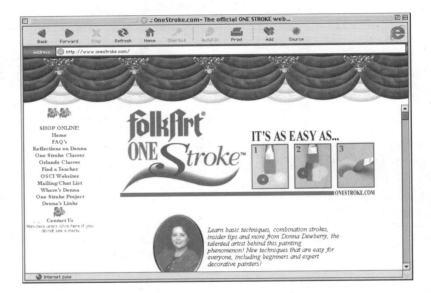

The Button bar (see Figure 2.5) contains buttons for common functions. They are similar to the ones described in the table above; the only difference is that the **Reload** button in Netscape is called **Refresh** in IE.

Figure 2.5
The Internet Explorer
button bar.

Browsing the Web

When you want to visit a Web page, you type the Web page address into the Address box (Location Box) and hit **Enter** (or **Return** on a Macintosh). The Web page is then loaded into the browser window. Most Web pages contain links to other pages. Links come in many shapes—some are graphical buttons and others consist of text, which is usually colored and underlined. In addition to color, links provide other visual clues to help you identify them. For example, when you move your mouse cursor over a link (this action is called a "mouseover"), it usually turns into a pointing hand to let you know that you've found a clickable object.

Anatomy of a URL

A Web Address or URL (Uniform Resource Locator) is a unique way to identify an object on the Web, the same way an address is used to locate a house or a building. A URL for a Web page looks like this:

http://server.domain/path

The "http" part tells your computer that this is the address of a Web page, as opposed to some other kind of object. The server.domain portion of the URL identifies a specific computer on the Internet, and the path identifies a particular file on that computer. The simplest URL for a Web page looks something like this:

http://www.craftopia.com/

In this URL, the domain is craftopia.com; typically a domain represents a person, organization, or company. The "www" identifies a particular computer (known as a server) within the domain.

Here is another example from the same Web site:

http://www.craftopia.com/shop/projectstudio/magazine/dec00/

Again, the server is www, the domain is craftopia.com, and the path is /shop/projectstudio/ magazine/dec00/. A Web server is actually a computer just like your desktop computer, and it contains files that are organized in folders, just like you organize your own files. The path in the URL represents the folders containing the page you are viewing.

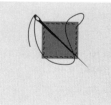

TIP

Sometimes, people will move or remove some pages from their Web sites. If you ever try to access a URL with a long path like the one above, and you get an error message saying that the page doesn't exist, you can start back at the home page, which is usually the first part of the URL, for example, **http://www.craftopia.com/**.

If you have wondered about the suffixes you see on URLs, here is what the principal ones mean:

Table 2.2
Common domain suffixes.

com	commercial organization
edu	educational institution
gov	government
mil	military
net	network
org	non-profit organization

These were the original definition of these suffixes, but some of them have become blurred over the years. You will also see suffixes for countries, like .ca for Canada, and .fr for France. New suffixes such as .biz and .info have recently been approved.

CAUTION
In this book, URLs are often part of the text, sometimes occurring at the ends of sentences. If you see a URL with a period at the end, this is the period that ends the sentence, and it is not part of the URL.

Managing Bookmarks

One of the most useful features of your Web browser is Bookmarks, known as Favorites in IE. Bookmarks offer you a way to save and organize the locations (URLs) of your favorite Web pages and make them easily available in a menu format. When you visit a Web site, and you know you will want to visit it again, you can set it as a bookmark.

I will show you how these work in both Netscape and Internet Explorer. I will be using Netscape version 4.7 and IE version 5.0 on a Macintosh computer; this feature may work slightly differently if you have a different version.

Bookmarks in Netscape

In Netscape, your bookmarks are kept in the **Bookmarks** menu. When you go to a Web site and you want to set a bookmark so that you can return easily, choose **Add Bookmark** from the **Bookmarks** menu (see Figure 2.6).

Figure 2.6

The Netscape Bookmarks drop-down menu appears when you click on Bookmarks in the browser menu bar.

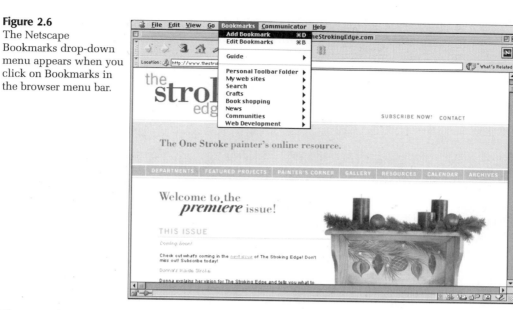

The next time you click the **Bookmarks** menu, the new bookmark appears at the bottom, and you simply select it at any time to go to that site (see Figure 2.7). The name that shows up in the menu is the title that you see at the top of the page.

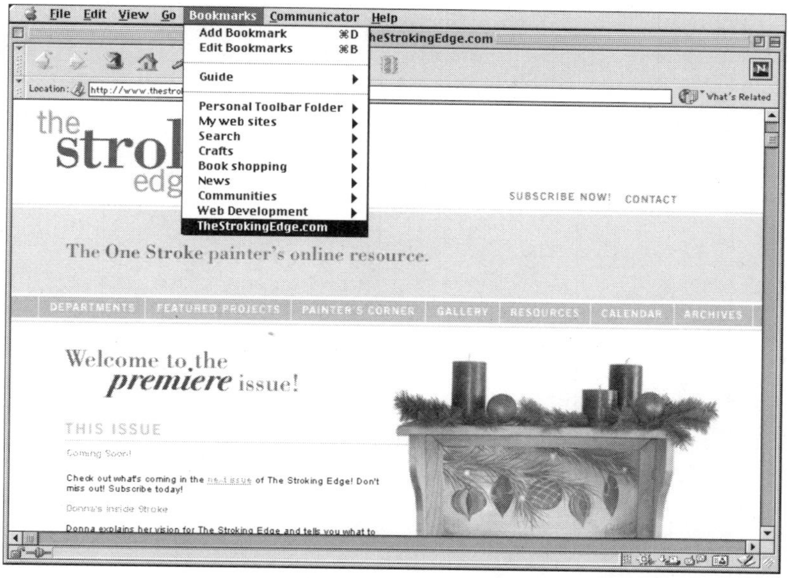

Figure 2.7

A new Bookmark, TheStrokingEdge.com, added in Netscape.

To organize your bookmarks, choose **Edit Bookmarks** from the **Bookmarks** menu. This opens a window containing your bookmarks (see Figure 2.8). To reorder your bookmarks, you can click and drag them up or down the list, and you can create folders (choose **New Folder** from the **File** menu) to classify your bookmark into categories. In this example, I could click and drag the new bookmark for The Stroking Edge into the Crafts folder.

To rename a bookmark, click the name and choose **Get Info** from the **Edit** menu. To delete a bookmark, click its name and hit **Delete** on your keyboard.

Figure 2.8
The Netscape Bookmarks window showing Bookmarks saved in specially created folders.

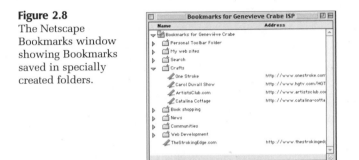

In addition to the bookmark menu, there is also a toolbar called the Personal Toolbar. To display it in your Netscape window, choose **Personal Toolbar** under **Show** in the **View** menu. The toolbar appears under the Location bar (see Figure 2.9).

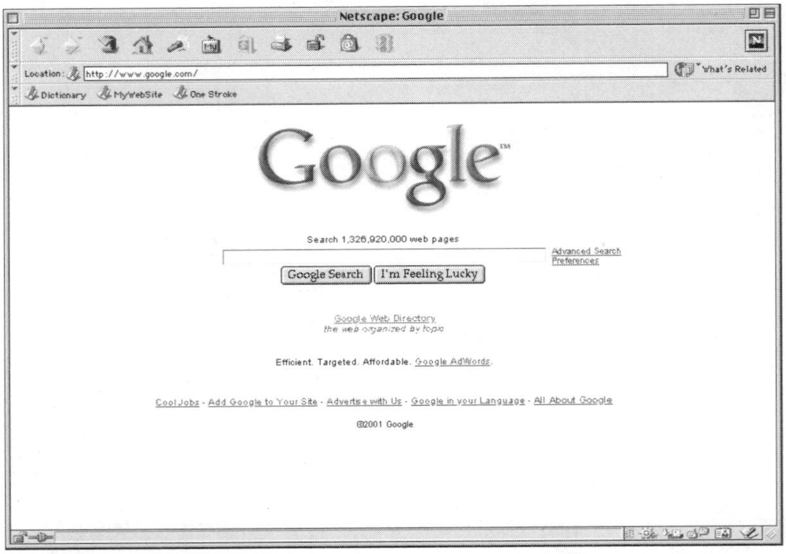

Figure 2.9
The Personal Toolbar (shown in Netscape) is just beneath the Location bar.

Links of your choosing can be added to this bar by going to the Web site, then dragging the icon at the left of the location onto the bar (see Figure 2.10). Once you have done this, you can go to that Web site any time by simply clicking the link in the toolbar.

Figure 2.10
Adding a link to the Personal Toolbar: Click on the icon, drag it to the Personal Toolbar, and release it.

You can organize the links on your Personal Toolbar just like your other bookmarks. In your Bookmarks window (see Figure 2.8), the folder called **Personal Toolbar Folder** is where you'll find your toolbar bookmarks. Open the folder by clicking the triangle next to the folder, and then you can manipulate the bookmarks like any others.

TIP
Use the Personal Toolbar for those links you use most often, such as your favorite search engine.

Favorites in Internet Explorer

In IE, your bookmarks are kept in the **Favorites** menu. When you go to a Web site and you want to set a bookmark so that you can return easily, choose **Add Page to Favorites** from the **Favorites** menu (see Figure 2.11).

Figure 2.11
The Favorites drop-down menu in Internet Explorer.

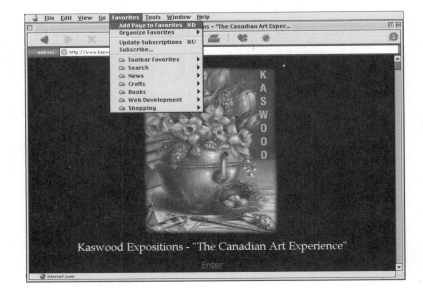

Kaswood Expositions - "The Canadian Art Experience"

The next time you click the **Favorites** menu, the new bookmark appears at the bottom, and you simply select it (click on it) at any time to go to that site (see Figure 2.12). The name that shows up in the menu is the title that you see at the top of the page.

Figure 2.12
A new link, Kaswood Exhibitions, added in Internet Explorer.

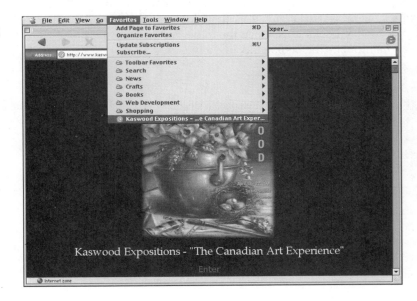

Kaswood Expositions - "The Canadian Art Experience"

To organize your bookmarks, choose **Organize Favorites** from the **Favorites** menu. This opens a window containing your bookmarks (see Figure 2.13). To reorder your bookmarks, you can click and drag the bookmarks up or down in the list, and you can create folders (choose **New Folder** under **Organize Favorites** in the **Favorites** menu) to classify your bookmarks into categories. In this example, I could drag the new bookmark for Kaswood Expositions into the Crafts folder.

To rename a bookmark, click the name and choose **Get Info** from the **File** menu. To delete a bookmark, click its name and hit **Delete** on your keyboard.

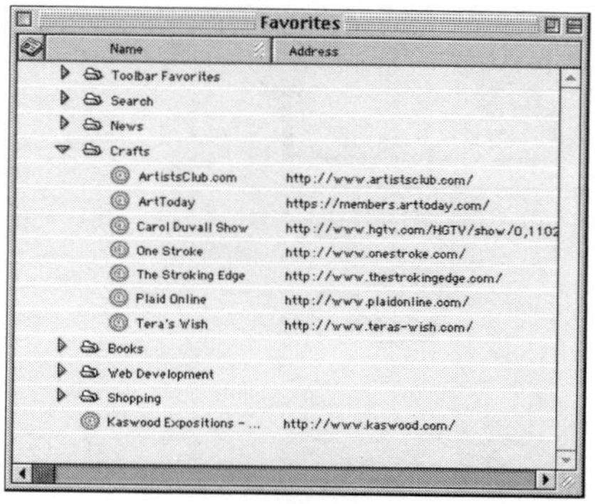

Figure 2.13
The Favorites window, showing Favorites saved in specially created folders.

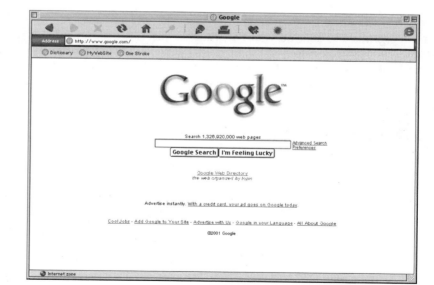

In addition to the Favorites menu, there is also a toolbar called the **Favorites Bar**. To display it in your IE window, choose **Favorites Bar** in the **View** menu. The toolbar appears under the Address bar (see Figure 2.14).

Figure 2.14
The Favorites bar is located just under the Address bar in Internet Explorer.

Links of your choosing can be added to this bar by going to the Web site, then dragging the icon at the left of the location onto the bar (see Figure 2.15) onto the Favorites Bar. Once you have done this, you can go to that Web site any time by simply clicking the link in the toolbar.

Figure 2.15
Adding a link to the Favorites bar: Click on the icon just before the URL, drag it to the Favorites Bar below, and release.

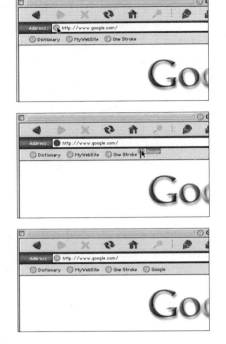

You can organize the links on your Favorites Bar just like your other bookmarks. In your Favorites window (see Figure 2.13), the folder called **Toolbar Favorites** is where your find your toolbar bookmarks. Open the folder by clicking the triangle next to the folder, and then you can manipulate the bookmarks like any others.

Web-Based E-Mail

In Chapter 1, we talked about using e-mail software. There are also e-mail accounts that are accessible using a Web browser instead of e-mail software. Many Web sites offer e-mail at no charge, because the cost is actually paid for by advertisers who add a tag at the end of each e-mail you send and display advertisements on the Web pages where you read your e-mail. Figure 2.16 shows a Yahoo! e-mail account I just created.

Figure 2.16
Yahoo! mail.

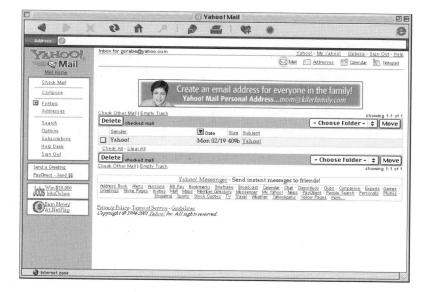

Many Web sites offer free e-mail—here are a few examples:

Table 2.3
Sites that offer free e-mail:

Yahoo!	http://mail.yahoo.com/
HotMail	http://www.hotmail.com/
Canada.com	http://canada.com/
BigFoot	http://www.bigfoot.com/

One of the advantages of getting one of these e-mail accounts is that they are accessible from any Web browser. For example, if you are traveling, you can go to a library or an Internet café and access your e-mail. Some offer e-mail forwarding, so you can have your messages forwarded to your regular account, and if you move from one service provider to another, the Web-based e-mail address remains the same. Also, with these free accounts, you can set up several e-mail addresses to use for different purposes. In particular, you can use a free account for participating on public discussion lists, while reserving your personal e-mail account (the one you get from your Internet service provider) for friends and family.

A word of caution about free e-mail accounts—sometimes the service can be unavailable because of technical problems, and it can be difficult to get in touch with someone in charge to find out how long the outage will be. Also, mail sent to you during the outage might be lost. With your ISP, you are a paying customer, so you have access to technical support to resolve these issues.

Section II
Researching Online

"Knowledge is of two kinds. We know a subject ourselves, or we know where we can find information upon it."

—Samuel Johnson

3

Searching the Web

As I mentioned earlier, the Web consists of hundreds of millions of pages of information, which begs the question, how do you find things? You might get Web addresses from your friends, then follow links from there to visit other sites, but finding everything you need or want this way is a hit-or-miss proposition.

Searching for information on the Internet is a lot like detective work, and like any good detective, you want to make sure you have the right tools. Your tools are called search engines and Web directories.

Search Engines and Web Directories

A search engine is a Web site that uses automated software programs to scour the Web for information. These programs travel the Web from page to page, following links and indexing information as they go. The resulting index is what you are searching when you use a search engine. Some search engines are better than others, depending on how many Web pages they have indexed, how good their indexing scheme is, and how often they revisit sites. Examples of search engines are AltaVista at **http://www.altavista.com/** (see Figure 3.1) and Google at **http://www.google.com/**.

A Web directory, on the other hand, is more like a library catalogue, where lists of Web sites are classified by category. You can use a Web directory in two different ways: You can browse through the categories, or you can use the search feature to look for something specific. The best known Web directory is Yahoo! at **http://www.yahoo.com/**; AltaVista and Google also contain Web directories. We will look at all of them later in the chapter.

If you ask whether it's better to use a search engine or a directory, the answer is…it depends. They are both very useful. Results from a directory are usually better organized, but you usually get more results from a search engine. Also note that some of the items you see on a search results page are paid listings as opposed to actual search results. These are usually offset from the rest, though, either off to the side or at the top.

Section II Researching Online

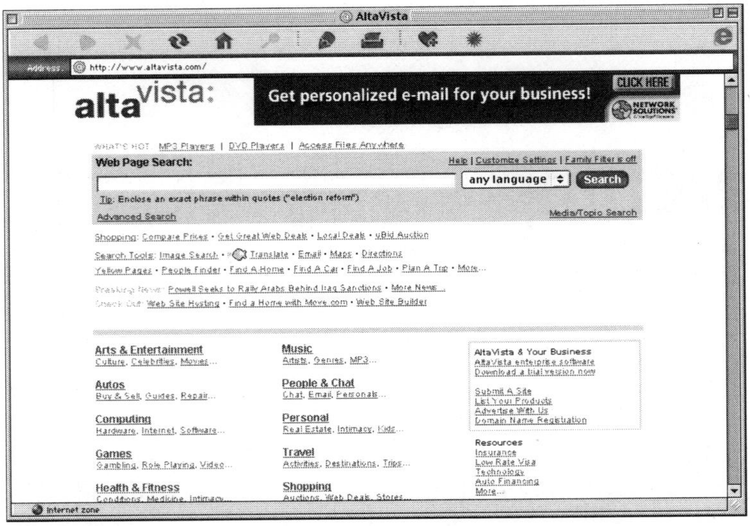

Figure 3.1
AltaVista is a popular
search engine.

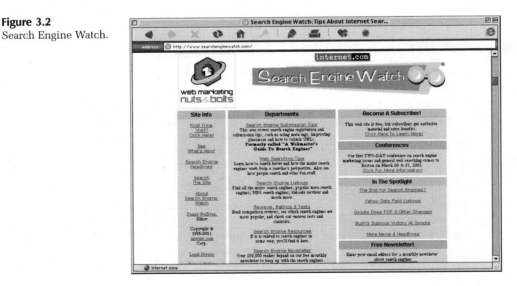

If you are interested in search engines and want to keep up with news in this area, you can visit the Search Engine Watch Web site at **http://www.searchenginewatch.com/** (see Figure 3.2).

Figure 3.2
Search Engine Watch.

Tips for Effective Searching

There are a lot of ways in which you can improve the quality of your search results. There are some differences between search engines, so if you don't get the results you expect, check the tips that are given on each search site. I will focus on techniques that work with most search engines. The examples in this section use the AltaVista search engine, **http://www.altavista.com/**.

The most important thing to remember is to use words that are as specific as possible. For example, if you are interested in decorative painting, search for "tole painting" or "decorative painting" rather then just "painting." If you don't find what you are looking for in a specific search, you can then try the broader terms.

When you simply enter two words like this:

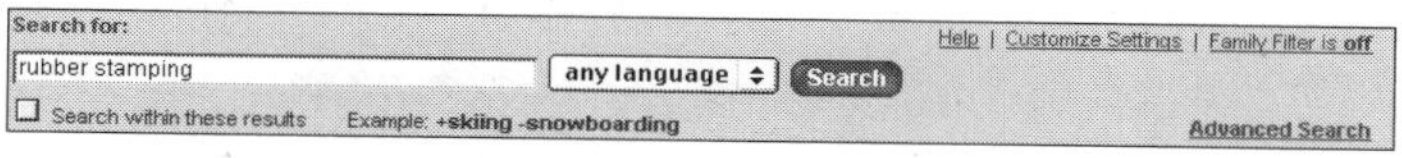

AltaVista will look for pages that contain one or the other of these words, but it will list pages that contain both words at the top of the results page (see Figure 3.3).

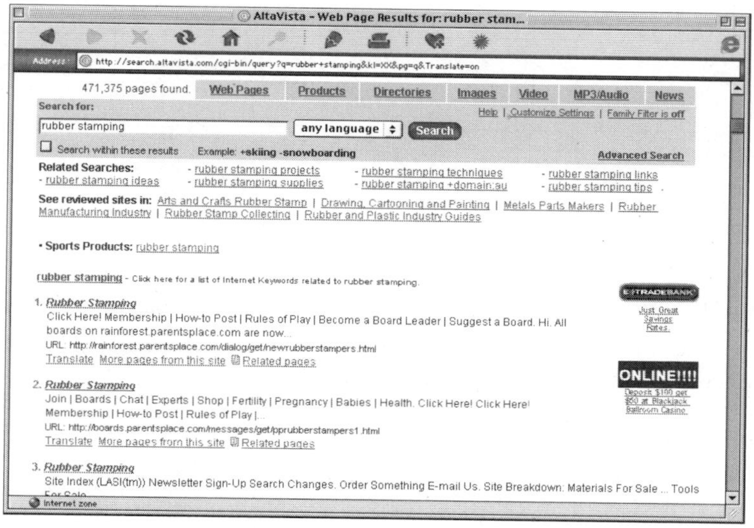

Figure 3.3
Results from an AltaVista search for the words *rubber stamping* if found alone or together in a page.

As you can see in the upper left-hand corner of Figure 3.3, AltaVista found more than 470,000 pages containing either the word "rubber" or the word "stamping." You can narrow down your results in two ways. First, if you put a plus sign in front of the words, the search will return only those pages that contain both words.

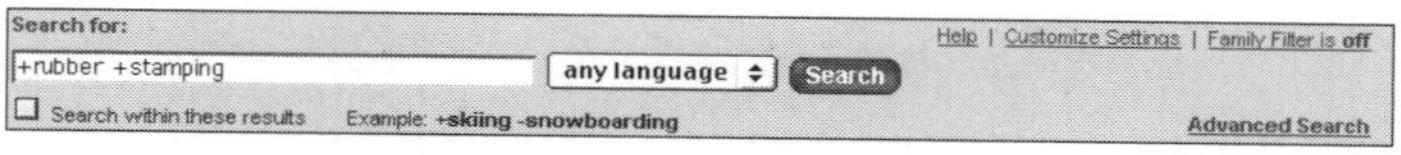

In the upper left-hand corner of Figure 3.4, we can see that this search has found around 55,000 pages.

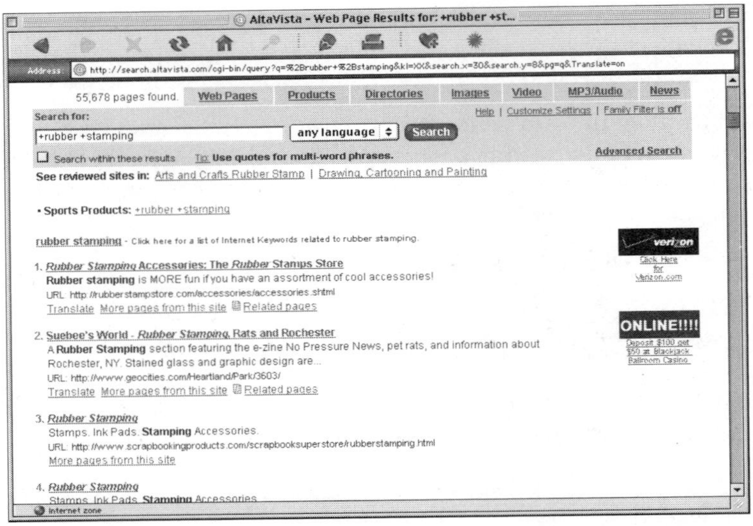

Figure 3.4
The results of an AltaVista search for +*rubber* +*stamping*, meaning both words must be found in the same page.

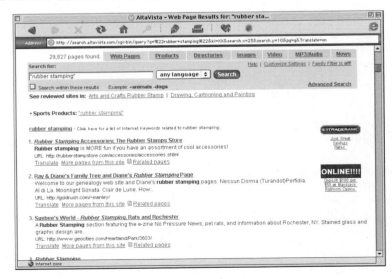

To narrow the results even further, we can enclose the two words in quotes, like this:

This will cause the search engine to return only pages that contain the phrase "*rubber stamping*"—that is, the two words together as a phrase.

Figure 3.5 shows that we now have narrowed down the results to under 30,000.

Figure 3.5
The results of an AltaVista search for "*rubber stamping*" as a phrase to be found in a page.

If you are looking for places to buy rubber stamping supplies, you can try this:

```
Search for:
+"rubber stamping" +store          any language ▼   Search
☐ Search within these results   Example: +skiing -snowboarding
                                          Help | Customize Settings | Family Filter is off
                                                          Advanced Search
```

The number of results has now gone down even more (see Figure 3.6).

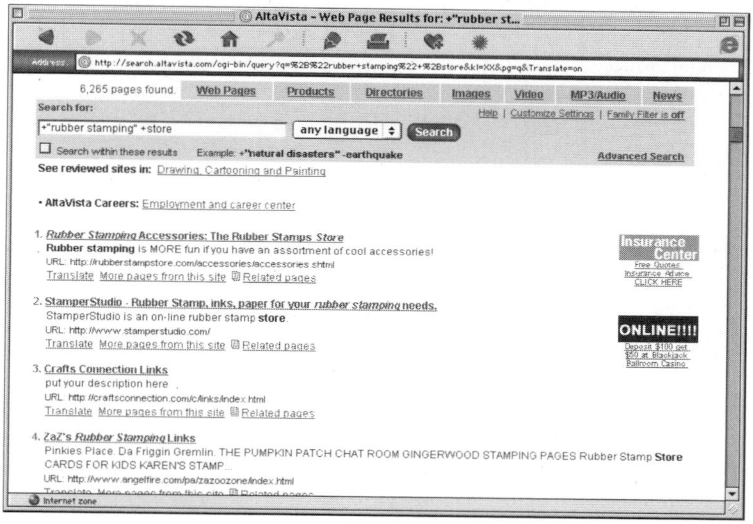

Figure 3.6
The results of an
AltaVista search for
+"rubber stamping"
+store, meaning the
phrase "rubber
stamping" plus the
word "store" must be
found in the same page.

Now, say you wanted to exclude some words from your search. For example, to continue with
our rubber stamp theme, suppose you were interested in rubber stamping, but you wanted
information on things other than scrapbooking, which is one of the major uses for stamps
nowadays. Then you would use the minus sign to exclude words:

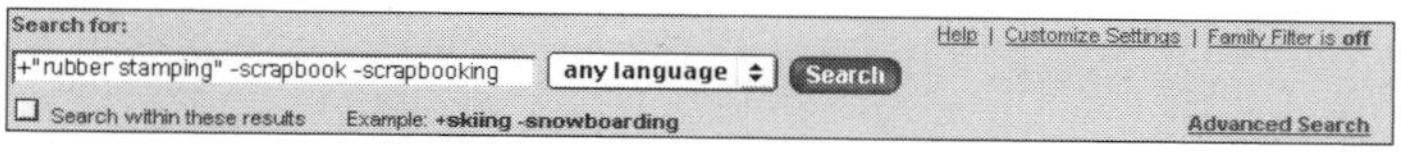

```
Search for:
+"rubber stamping" -scrapbook -scrapbooking   any language ▼   Search
☐ Search within these results   Example: +skiing -snowboarding
                                          Help | Customize Settings | Family Filter is off
                                                          Advanced Search
```

The results you will get (see Figure 3.7) are pages that contain the phrase "rubber stamping" but do not contain either the word "scrapbook" or "scrapbooking." This exclusion feature is very useful for narrowing down a search.

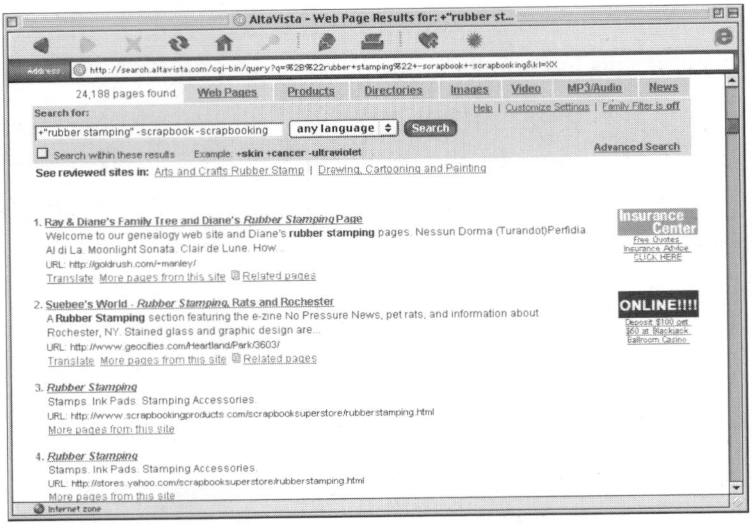

Figure 3.7
Results of an AltaVista search for +*"rubber stamping"* −*scrapbook* −*scrapbooking*, meaning the phrase "rubber stamping" must be found in the page but the words "scrapbook" and "scrapbooking" must not be found in the page.

You can also use an asterisk as a wildcard character. The previous search could have been entered like this:

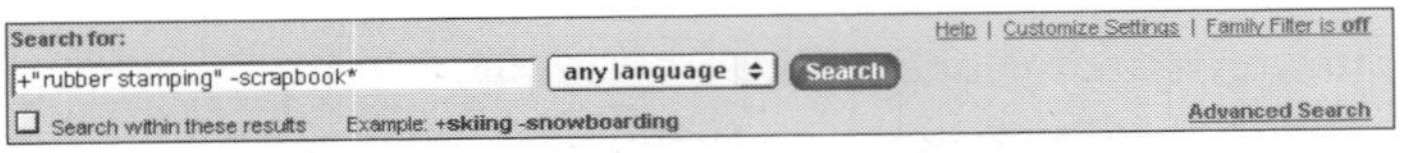

and this would have excluded all words that begin with "scrapbook," such as scrapbooks, scrapbooking, and so on.

Table 3.1 shows a few more examples:

Table 3.1
Search Examples

"making papier-mâché"	Instead of entering just "papier-mâché" and getting lots of pages about what to do with papier-mâché objects, adding the word "making" will narrow down the results to information about making your own.
+"glass painting" – window	This will focus your search on glass painting on surfaces other than windows.
"Carol Duvall"	If you are searching for Web sites about a particular person, always enclose the whole name in quotes.
+crochet + "free projects"	Search for sites about crochet, but narrow down the search to those that offer free projects.
+scrapbooking +supplies +california	Use a search like this to focus your search on sites that are in a particular location.
quilt*	Specifying different forms of the same word will expand your search. Using the wildcard means that the search will include all words that begin with "quilt," such as "quilting," "quilter," and so on.
+"decorative painting" – stencil	This is how you would search for sites on decorative painting using techniques other than stenciling.

More Search Sites

AltaVista is very popular, but there are many different search engines, each with different features. Here are a few you can try—you'll probably discover one that will become your favorite.

AskJeeves

http://www.ask.com/

AskJeeves (see Figure 3.8) is a terrific search engine for beginners, because you can ask questions in plain English. For example, I asked, "Where can I find free crochet patterns," and I got the results shown in Figure 3.9.

Figure 3.8
The AskJeeves
home page.

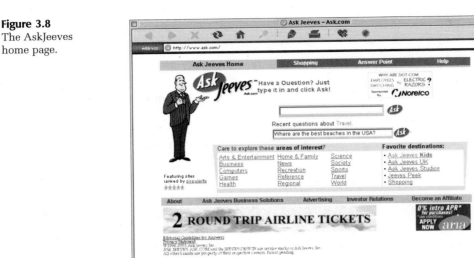

The first panel of results consists of a series of related questions that show how AskJeeves interpreted your initial question; some of these questions contain drop-down menus from which you can make a choice that most closely matches your question. If the results are not what you were looking for, you can try to reformulate your question.

Figure 3.9
An AskJeeves
results page.

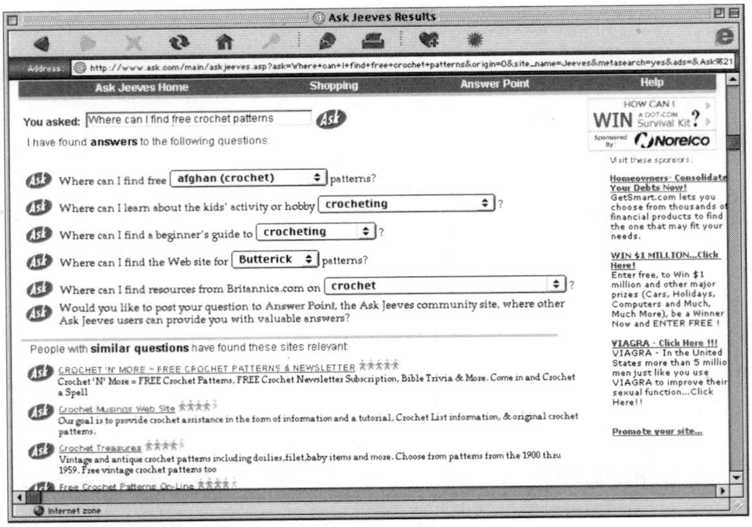

The second panel of the results page shows sites that people with similar questions have found relevant. You can see that in this case, there are definitely sites on this list that answer my question.

Google

http://www.google.com/

My favorite search site is Google, which has both a search engine at its main URL and a Web directory at **http://directory.google.com/** (see Figure 3.10).

Figure 3.10
The Google
search engine.

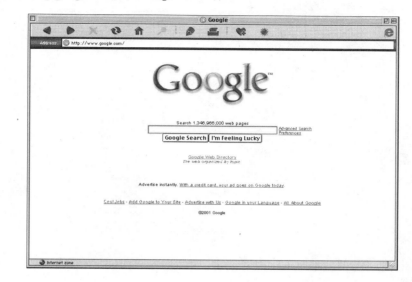

The Google search engine is great for its simplicity. Type one or more words in the box, click Google Search, and read the results. The search will return pages containing all the words you typed in. If you want more specific search options, click Advanced Search. The Advanced Search form (see Figure 3.11) enables you to perform complex searches without having to remember complex syntax.

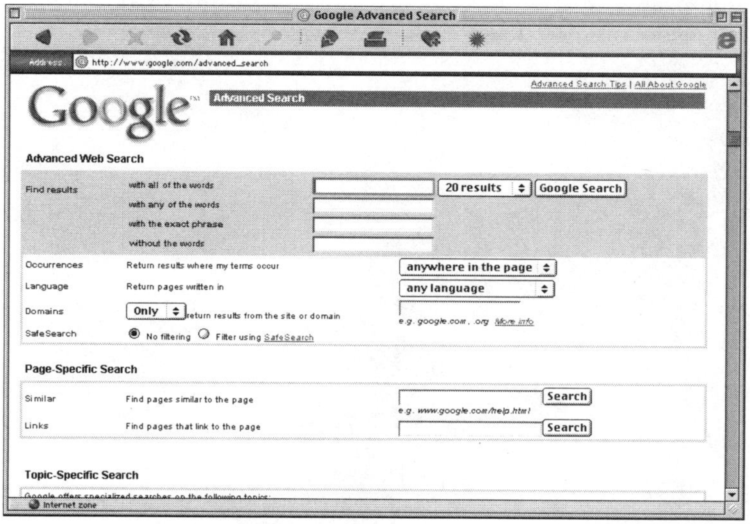

Figure 3.11
The Google Advanced
Search page.

In addition to the search engine, Goggle also has a Web directory (see Figure 3.12) where you can search for Web sites by category.

Figure 3.12
The Google Web
Directory page.

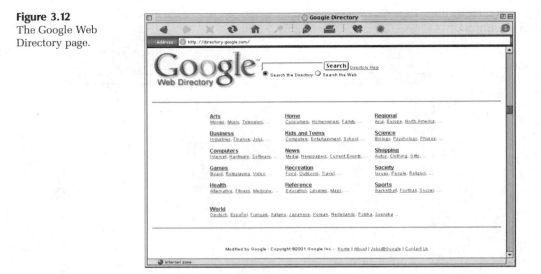

Yahoo!

http://www.yahoo.com/

Yahoo! is probably the best known Web directory (see Figure 3.13). Unlike the search engines that build their index using software, Yahoo! is organized by people who evaluate Web sites and then organize them into categories.

You can search this directory the same way you use search engines—it supports plus/minus signs and wildcards, but the search is restricted to the sites that have been put into the directory, which is a smaller number than the sites covered by search engines.

Figure 3.13
The Yahoo!
Web directory.

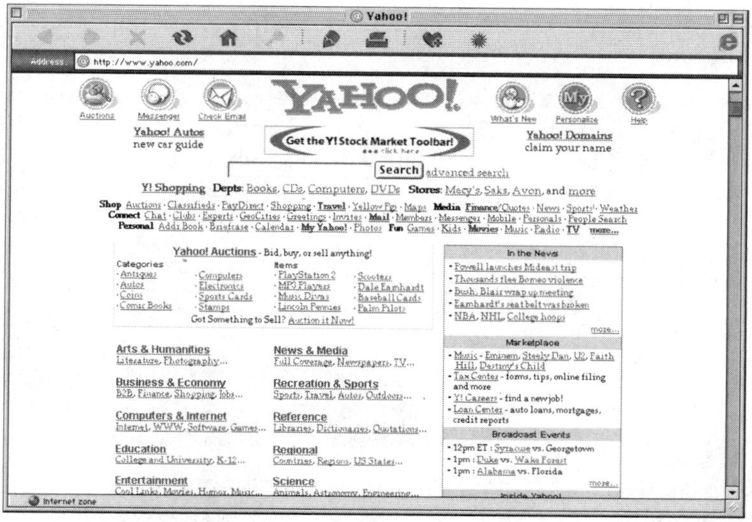

I like to use Web directories for browsing rather than searching. For examples, if I start by clicking "Art & Humanities," then "Crafts," I get the page shown in Figure 3.14. From here, you can go deeper into whatever category interests you.

Figure 3.14
The Crafts categories
page in the Yahoo!
Web directory.

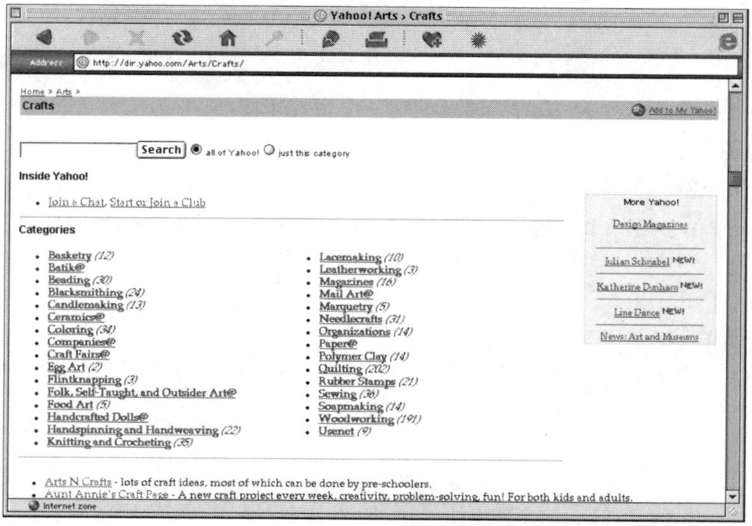

If you want to search Canadian sites, many of the search sites have Canadian equivalents:

>   Alta Vista: **http://www.altavista.ca/**
>   Yahoo: **http://www.yahoo.ca/**

About.com

http://about.com/

About.com (see Figure 3.15) is another site where you can search for information. This is actually a large community. When you search About.com, links to related pages on the About.com site are listed first, followed by results from other search sites. I'll describe About.com in more detail in Chapter 6 when we talk about online communities.

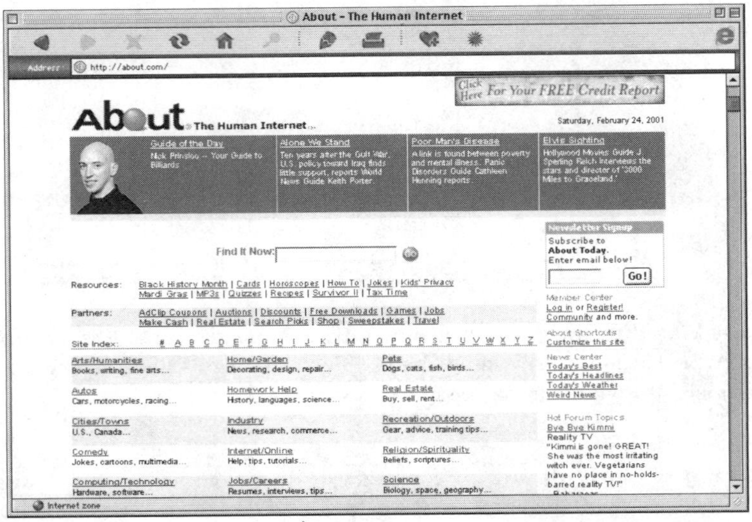

Figure 3.15
The About.com home page.

FindArticles

http://www.findarticles.com

If you want to search for magazine articles, you can try FindArticles. Figure 3.16 shows the results I got when I did a search on "scrapbooking."

Figure 3.16
FindArticles.com.

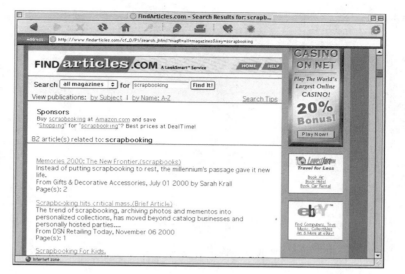

Sherlock

If your computer is a Macintosh, you have a wonderful built-in search tool called Sherlock that you can use to search the Internet. To bring up Sherlock, choose **Find** from the **File** menu in the Finder. Then, click the Internet channel button (the one that looks like a globe) and you get a list of search sites (see Figure 3.17).

Figure 3.17
The Sherlock
Internet Channel.

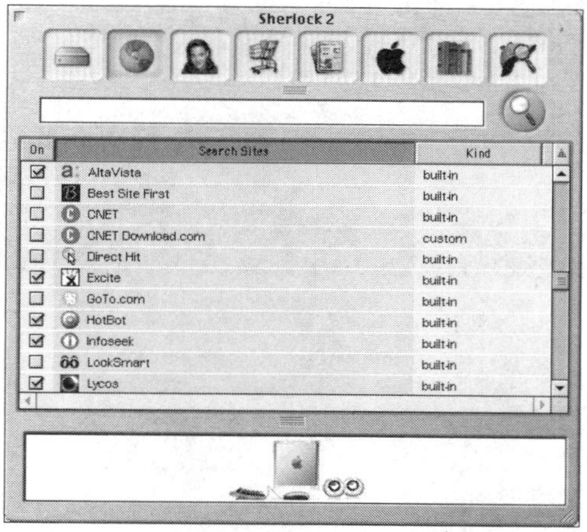

Use the checkboxes in the list to pick the search engines you want to use. If you enter your search words and click the magnifying glass, the top results from all the search engines will be listed in the window. In Figure 3.18, I did a search on "needlepoint."

Section II Researching Online

Figure 3.18
Sherlock search results.

To go to one of the sites, double-click the URL in the Sherlock window.

Craft-Specific Search Sites

Craft Solutions

http://craftsolutions.com

The Craft Solutions Web site (see Figure 3.19) is a search engine and directory specializing in crafts. You can search for craft shops, resources, or projects.

Figure 3.19
The Craft Solutions
home page.

Crafts Fair Online
http://www.craftsfaironline.com

The Crafts Fair Online Web site (see Figure 3.20) is a directory of thousands of crafts Web sites, including online craft malls, craft organizations, suppliers, listings of craft shows, craft publications, etc.

Figure3.20
The Crafts Fair Online
home page.

Other excellent sources of Web addresses are your craft magazines. Most magazines have their own Web sites (many are listed on the companion Web site associated with this book), and many articles and advertisements include URLs to companies' Web sites.

Section II Researching Online

4

Sparking
Your Creativity

As a crafter, you have specific supplies and tools that you use in your craft. In addition to that, there is an elusive ingredient called creativity.

As an artist or crafter, it is necessary to always come up with new ideas, and the Internet can be a great assistance in this search. The Internet gives you a window to the world right on your desk top, allowing you to visit art galleries, museums, craft shops, classrooms—in other words, many places where you can find inspiration.

Learning Online

There are a lot of ways to learn new things. You can read a book, take a class—or you can get on the Internet. Many Web sites offer information or training in a variety of subjects.

In some cases, the information is free. In other cases, such as in some training courses, you have to register and pay a fee (Just like any other site where you have to give out information, always check the privacy policy first to find out how they will treat the information they receive from you).

At its simplest, online training consists of a Web site containing a series of informative pages much like a book. At the other end of the spectrum, online training takes full advantage of all that the Internet has to offer by using animation, video, live interaction with instructors and other learners, and so on. Most online learning sites offer features that are somewhere between these two extremes.

For example, the Art Studio Chalkboard at **http://www2.evansville.edu/studiochalkboard/** from the University of Evansville offers lessons on the fundamentals of drawing that can be of use in many crafts. These lessons can be accessed at no charge for educational purposes. You can learn about perspective, shading, and more. Figure 4.1 shows the beginning of a lesson on linear perspective. You can click through several lessons, each one with links to reference materials in case you want to find out more about the subject.

Figure 4.1
A lesson on
perspective at Art
Studio Chalkboard.

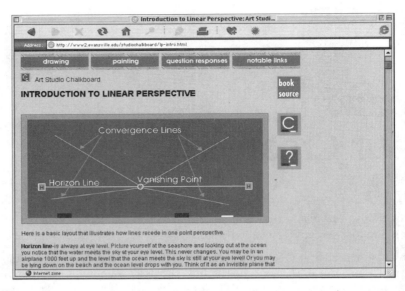

The American Needlepoint Guild offers its CyberWorkshops at **http://www.needlepoint.org/ CyberWorkshop/** (see Figure 4.2). These workshops are conducted by e-mail discussion list, with a teacher providing instructions and guidance and the students providing feedback and asking questions. A discussion list consists of a group of people with a common interest who communicate by sending e-mails to the group. In this case, the membership consists only of the students and the teacher for a particular class. The discussion list setting, which will be described in detail in Chapter 6, works very well for this type of learning, where students can progress at their own individual rates and at their own convenience. The cost of these workshops is similar to what you might pay for a conventional class.

Figure 4.2
The American
Needlepoint Guild
offers online
"CyberWorkshops".

Quilt University at **http://www.quiltuniversity.com/** offers several quilting classes (see Figure 4.3). Once you register, you are given a password to access class materials and an e-mail discussion list where you can ask questions. In addition, there is a public message board where anyone can participate and ask questions about classes. A public message board is a Web page where people can post messages to communicate with each other.

Figure 4.3
The Quilt University
home page.

Want to learn about a new craft technique? The headline on eHow at **http://eHow.com/** (see Figure 4.4) reads, "How to do just about everything." As I write this, eHow.com contains 15,000 how-to solutions.

Section II Researching Online

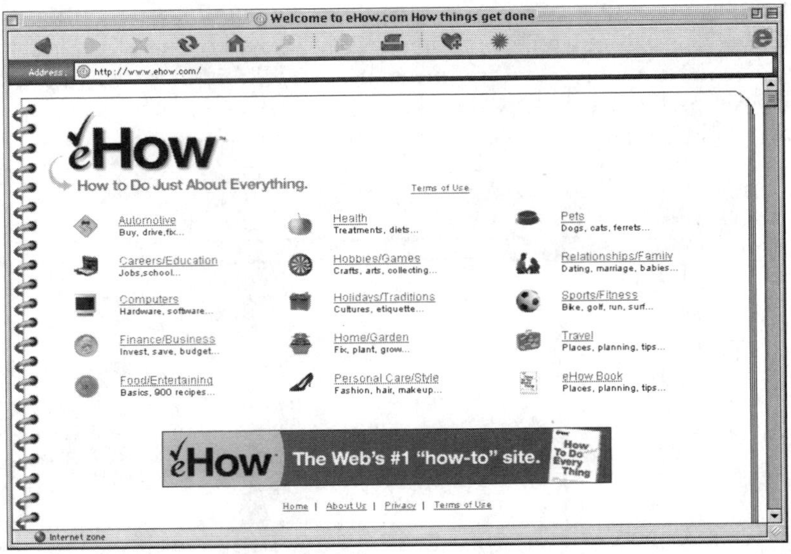

Figure 4.4
The eHow.com home page points you toward thousands of topics.

Figure 4.5 shows the Crafts section of eHow.com. What you see in the screen shot is just the tip of the iceberg; I had to scroll down eighteen screens to get to the bottom of this page.

TIP
If you are looking at a long Web page, you can use the **Find** command under the **Edit** menu to search for something specific.

Figure 4.5
The eHow.com Crafts section—this is just the beginning!

Once you click on a particular item (called an "eHow"), here is what you get:

▶ Instructions, with a link to a printable copy

▶ Links to related eHows

▶ A shopping list of supplies with suggested suppliers

▶ Additional tips from other users

▶ A link to "ask an expert" for more information

▶ Other related links

▶ A list of related books

Right now, online training on the Internet is somewhat limited. As more people get high-speed connections to the Internet, though, you will begin to see more extensive online training that uses live video and audio to create virtual classrooms. The teaching of crafting skills will benefit greatly from these new technologies.

Just as in live classes you might take, you might want to know something about the instructor before you sign up. Look for a Web page with this information; it may even have a link to the instructor's own Web site, if there is one. You can also ask whether there are testimonials from students to help you judge the quality of the classes.

Free Projects

If you are looking for ideas for new projects, many sites offer a variety of free projects covering a large number of different crafts. You can use your search engine and search for "free craft projects" to find many such sites.

TIP

I have found that on some Web pages, the text is very small and difficult to read. In your browser, you can increase the size of the text on the page. In Netscape, choose **Increase Font Size** from the **View** menu; in Internet Explorer, choose one of the options in **Text Zoom** under the **View** menu.

One such site is Home & Garden Television at **http://www.hgtv.com/** (see Figure 4.6), where you can find project sheets for many of the projects that have been shown on their shows. Even if you don't get HGTV, you can browse through the projects and find something of interest.

Figure 4.6
The HGTV Web site offers patterns and project instructions.

Finding Projects

On the main HGTV page, click **HGTV Show List** (upper right), then click the name of a show, such as *Our Place*. You then get the page for the show (see Figure 4.7).

Figure 4.7
HGTV's *Our Place* television show.

In the search box, enter what you want to look for. In this example, I enter "Decoupage" and click the **Search** button. You get the results shown in Figure 4.8.

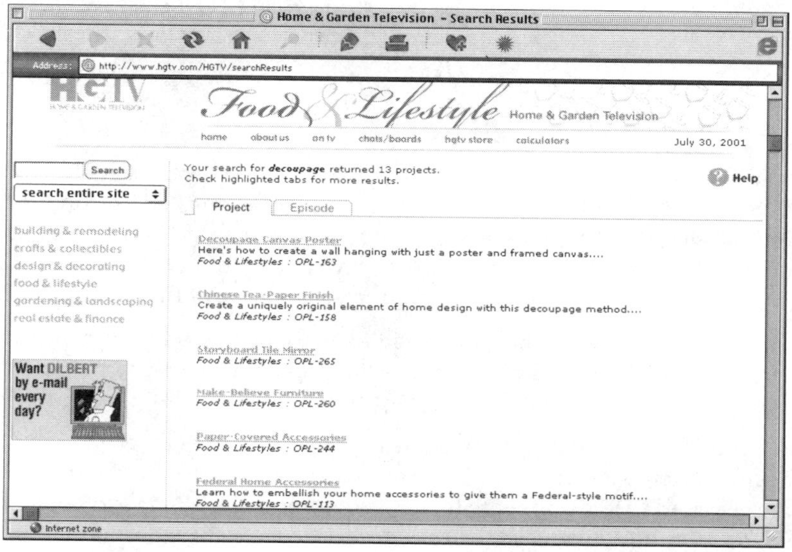

Figure 4.8
List of Decoupage projects shown on Our Place.

Click one of the projects to see the Project sheet (see Figure 4.9). This page includes instructions and photos, as well as links to related information on the HGTV Web site. There is also a **Print Version** link that will take you to a page with all the projects instructions and pictures, but without a lot of the extraneous graphics.

Figure 4.9
A project page on HGTV.

TIP

Many sites that feature projects will offer a "Printer friendly version," a separate page with the instructions and project-related images, but without the Web site's banner graphics. These print more quickly and will be easier to read.

Saving Project Instructions

If you want to save the project instructions, you have several options. The first is simply to print the Web page or the printer-friendly version if there is one. The second is to bookmark the URL and return later; the danger here is that the Web site might change—the project page might be moved or removed. The third option is to save a copy of the Web page on your hard disk; this way, you can save a whole collection of projects and print them only when you need to.

You might want to check what rights you have to the project. You may have the right to print a copy or save it to your hard disk and use the project instructions for personal use only. You'll find more information about this in Chapter 5.

My favorite way to save project pages is to convert them to Portable Document Format (PDF) using Adobe Acrobat software. PDF is a standard for electronic distribution of documents, and anyone can read PDF documents by using the free Adobe Acrobat Reader application, which can be found at **http://www.adobe.com/products/acrobat/readermain.html**.

If you have a Macintosh computer, you can use Jim Walker's PrintToPDF utility, which can be found at **http://www.jwwalker.com/**. It works like any other printer device; once you install it, it shows up in the Chooser (see Figure 4.10). After you select it in the Chooser, you can go to your browser and print a Web page; instead of it coming out on your printer, it comes out as a PDF document on your hard disk.

Once the document is on your hard disk and you have the Acrobat Reader installed, you can open it and look at it on the screen or print it out whenever you wish.

Figure 4.10
PrintToPDF.

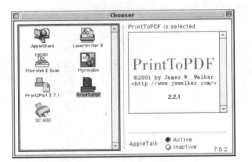

For Windows, there is a similar program called Print2PDF, part of a package called 602Pro Print Pack from Software602 Inc., which can be found at **http://www.software602.com/**. Neither of these programs is free, but both are very affordable.

Finding Inspiration

When you are involved in crafts, it's important to have sources for fresh ideas. Craft magazines, libraries, and museums can offer some new ideas, but the Internet opens up many new horizons.

The Creative Internet

Creativity seminars are very popular in the craft business community, but they can be very expensive. There are many creativity resources on the Web for you to tap into. You can use a search engine to look for them and then decide what appeals to you. Here are a few examples.

Creative Think

http://www.creativethink.com

Creativity often involves changing the way you think about things. The Creative Think Web site is the home of Roger von Oech's "Creative Whack®," a series of creative ideas to make you think in different ways about whatever you are doing (see Figure 4.11).

Figure 4.11
Roger von Oech's
Creative Think
Web site.

"Anyone can look for fashion in a boutique or history in a museum. The creative explorer looks for history in a hardware store and fashion in an airport."

—Bob Wieder

Tera's Wish

http://www.teras-wish.com/

Tera Leigh is well known in the crafting world for her many articles on creativity. Her Web site, Tera's Wish (see Figure 4.12), was my inspiration for this chapter. Creativity can be a very elusive thing, and the Internet contains a wealth of resources on the creative process.

Figure 4.12
The home page
of Tera's Wish.

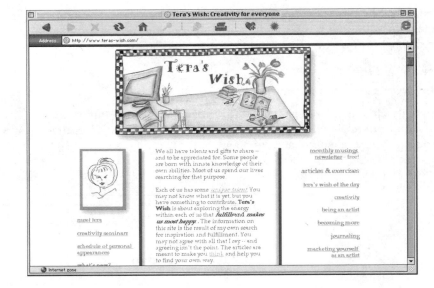

The following article by Tera Leigh was written for painters, but it can easily apply to all artists and crafters. In it, she suggests many Web sites where you can find information on creativity.

The Creative Internet
by Tera Leigh

Every painter experiences a creative slump from time to time. The Internet can be a wonderful resource for creative and inspiring information to get you back on track! From resource sites with articles and definitions, to sites offering online workshops and exercises, you are sure to find something to help.

Three years ago, I started my own site on creativity called Tera's Wish. (**http://www.teras-wish.com/**) We have been amazed at the growth of the site and the growing interest in creativity from painters around the world. Through that site, I have had the privilege to get to visit many online sites on creativity, and I want to share some of my favorites.

For many artists, Julia Cameron's book "The Artist's Way" is the "bible" of creativity. If you have been challenged to get through the book, you can join online with other artists at **http://www.minorkey.com/aw.html**. Join a group going through the book and talk via email or on chats. These groups are not limited to painters, but that often adds to the value of the group and the perspectives they give. There are several other Artist Way sites online.

The National Center for Creativity has an informative site at **http://www.creativesparks.org/ index2.html**. This site includes articles, wonderful quotes about creativity, a seminar listing, and reading list information. At **http://www.jpb.com/creative/creative.html** you will find an article on 10 Steps for Boosting Creativity. A teacher named Leslie Owen Wilson has put her research on creativity online, including articles, links, exam questions, and exercises on her site at **http://www.uwsp.edu/acad/educ/lwilson/creativ/**.

You'll find a site chock full of creative inspiration at **http://www.creative-edge.org/ btwota.htm** (be sure to read the Beginning the Way of the Arts articles), as well as at **http:// www.bemorecreative.com/cm/index.html** and then visit Adventures in Creativity, an online magazine at **http://www.volusia.com/creative/mag1.htm**.

The American Creativity Association (ACA) is a non-profit organization dedicated to promoting a creative society by (1) increasing awareness of the importance of creativity to society and (2) encouraging the development of personal and professional creativity. You'll find information about this group at **http://amcreativityassoc.org/**. Another exciting site is the Creativity Web. Resources are numerous and include books, software, and techniques. Additional resources are included to stimulate your thinking: quotations, affirmations, and humor. This site is located at: **http://members.ozemail.com.au/~caveman/Creative/index2.html/**.

At the wonderful Creative Inspiration site (**http://www.geocities.com/SoHo/7795/ main.html**), you will find articles about creativity and crafting, writing, needlework, and more.

One of the largest, if not the largest, resource site on the net about Creativity is **http://creativity.net/**—the Creativity Café. Finally, be sure to visit the Creative Aerobics site at **http://www.nutscape.com/creativity/html/indexx.htm**. The author provides a variety of fun and inspiring projects and exercises to get creativity flowing.

Tera Leigh is an artist and author living in the San Francisco Bay area. She has written the North Light "Complete Book of Decorative Painting" and is a columnist for PaintWorks and Decorative Artist's Workbook magazines. You can visit her Web site at **http://www.teraleigh.com/***.

Crafty Inspiration

You can find inspiration by seeing what other crafters are doing. Since many crafters are now selling online, you can visit their Web sites and find out what they are up to. Use your favorite search engine to look for the kind of items you are interested in, or, if you want to browse, you can go to a Web directory such as Google and look for Crafts in the Shopping section. companion Web site for this book contains many Web links for decorative painting and needlecraft artists.

If you are into scrapbooking, the Scrapbook Canada Web site at **http://www.scrapbookcanada.com/** (see Figure 4.13) has an area called the Scrapbook Hall of Fame, where people can share scrapbook pages. This can be a great source of inspiration for your own scrapbooks.

Figure 4.13
Scrapbook
Hall of Fame.

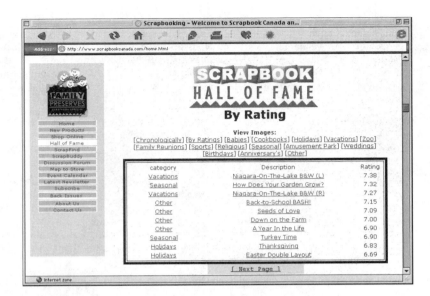

Nowadays, most craft-related television shows have their own Web sites. For example, Carol Duvall of *The Carol Duvall Show* on HGTV, has a Web site (see Figure 4.14) at **http://www.hgtv.com/** that includes instruction pages for all the projects presented on her show.

Figure 4.14
The companion
Web site to *The Carol
Duvall Show.*

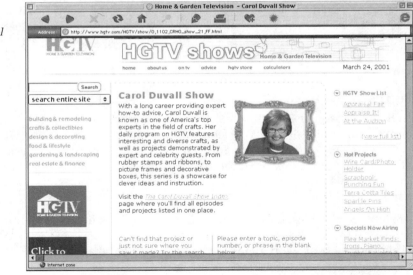

In Canada, the Web site for the *Sue Warden Craftscapes* television show is at
http://www.suewarden.com/ (see Figure 4.15) and includes an archive of all her quick-and-easy
projects, plus additional crafting tips.

Figure 4.15
The companion Web
site for *Sue Warden
Craftscapes.*

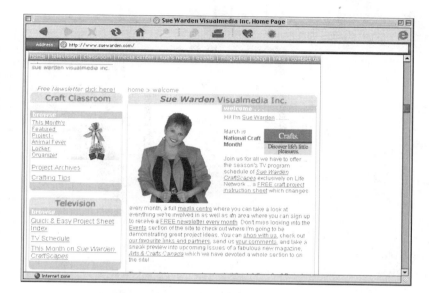

Web sites that accompany crafting shows usually contain resources related to the people and
projects they feature. You can find the URLs for more television shows on the companion
Web site. Also, the URL for a television show is usually displayed on the screen at the end
of the show.

Most craft magazines also have their own Web sites, and these sites often include Web-only
features such as extra projects, tips, contests, and e-mail newsletters. Check your favorite
magazines—if there is a Web site, the URL is probably printed on the front cover.

In addition to Web sites that are connected to paper magazines, there are also e-zines, magazines
that exist only online. Electronic magazines are much less expensive to distribute than print
magazines, so they can cover topics that have a much smaller audience than the magazines you
find in your newsstand. Some are free, but others charge a subscription fee just like paper
magazines. Here are a few examples.

Netcrafts Online
http://www.netcrafts.com/

This site offers some of the same features you find in print magazines, including patterns and
tips (see Figure 4.16).

Section II Researching Online

Figure 4.16
The home page of
Netcrafts Online e-zine.

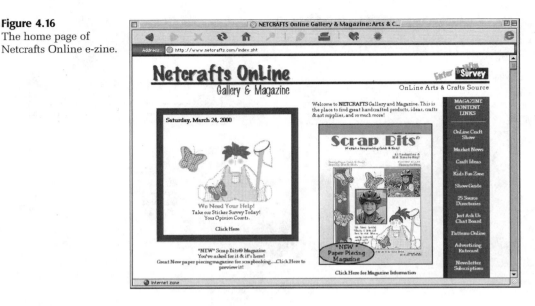

The Stroking Edge

http://www.thestrokingedge.com/

This e-zine is published by Donna Dewberry and devoted to her One Stroke painting technique. Although it includes some of the things you might find in a print magazine—such as project instructions—this e-zine takes advantage of the online medium to include live chats with Dewberry and streaming video clips (see Figure 4.17).

Figure 4.17
The home page of The
Stroking Edge e-zine.

Virtual Travel

Inspiration can come from obvious places—and some not-so-obvious ones. If you are lucky enough to live in a city that has tourist attractions like museums, you know that they are wonderful sources of inspiration. Now, thanks to the Internet, you can visit these places all over the world from the comfort of your own home.

For example, flowers are one of the most popular subjects for stitching, painting, and other crafts. Gardens can be a wonderful inspiration, but you don't always have the time or the opportunity to visit real gardens. How about visiting gardens on the Internet? Do a search on "gardens" and you will come up with some wonderful sites such as the Brooklyn Botanic Garden's Web site at **http://www.bbg.org/**, where you can take a virtual tour of the gardens (see Figure 4.18).

Figure 4.18
You can take a virtual tour of the Brooklyn Botanic Garden online.

A number of Web sites specialize in specific types of flowers. If you are looking for a particular one, search for the specific flower name. For example, I did a search on "orchid" and found many sites, including the Orchid Photo Page at **http://www.orchidworks.com/,** which contains more than 300 stunning photographs. You can see an example in Figure 4.19.

Figure 4.19
Find more than 300 photos at the Orchid Photo Page.

Museums can be an exciting source of inspiration, and now, with the Internet, you are no longer limited by local availability. Many museums around the world have Web sites that enable you to browse through their collections.

The Louvre in Paris is probably the most famous museum in the world.

Its Web site, at **http://www.louvre.fr/** (see Figure 4.20), has a multi-lingual interface and includes 3-D virtual tours of many of the galleries, including the Salle des Etats (see Figure 4.21), which houses its most famous painting, the Mona Lisa.

Figure 4.20
The Louvre museum Web site.

Figure 4.21
At the Louvre Web site, you may "tour" the Salle des Etats, home of the Mona Lisa.

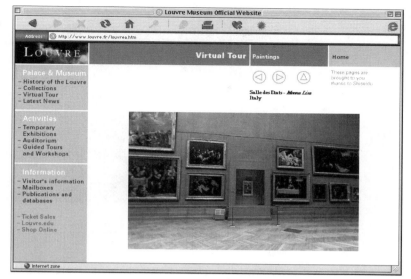

Section II Researching Online

Closer to home, the National Gallery of Art Web site, at **http://www.nga.gov/** (see Figure 4.22), includes some very impressive virtual tours. These use Apple's QuickTime software; just follow the instructions on the Web site to install it. If you don't have QuickTime, you can still take the tour using still images instead of the 3D interface.

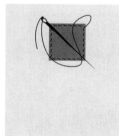

TIP

Once in a while, when you visit a Web site, you will be told that you need a special "plug-in" to view the content of the Web pages. A plug-in is a small software program that adds extra capabilities to a software program such as your Web browser—for example, the ability to view certain kinds of movies.

When a plug-in is required and you don't already have it, there will usually be a button on the Web page that will link you to a site where you will find instructions to install the plug-in for free.

Figure 4.22
The home page of the
National Gallery of Art
in Washington, D.C.

These tours (see Figure 4.23) allow you to navigate through the exhibitions. Within the tour window, you can click on a painting to see a close up and read information about it.

Figure 4.23
A view of a National
Gallery of Art
virtual tour.

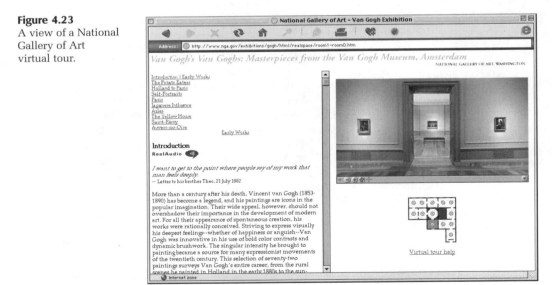

Similarly, the National Gallery of Canada Web site, at **http://national.gallery.ca/** (see Figure 4.24) has an area called CyberMuse that includes virtual tours of the galleries (see Figure 4.25).

Figure 4.24
The home page of
the National Gallery
of Canada in Ottawa,
Ontario.

Figure 4.25
Taking a virtual tour
at the National Gallery
of Canada.

Inspiration for Kids

There are many Web sites that specialize in crafts for kids. They're fun for children to use themselves, and they are also a great source of ideas for parents, teachers, child care workers, and anyone else who spends time with children.

ArtEdventures

http://www.sanford-artedventures.com/

Sanford's ArtEdventures (see Figure 4.26) offers projects for kids, students, and teachers, organized into four areas:

▶ Create Art includes artistic activities and techniques.

▶ Study Art contains a timeline of art and a glossary.

▶ Play Art Games features a variety of games and teacher resources.

▶ Teach Art offers lesson plans for teachers.

Figure 4.26
The home page of Sanford's ArtEdventures Web site.

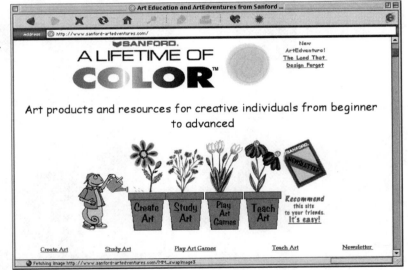

Crayola

http://www.crayola.com/

Crayola has a wonderful site for kids called Crayola Creativity Central (see Figure 4.27). The Inspiring Ideas section alone contains a huge collection of projects, which the company claims is the "world's largest collection of inspiring ideas." The Card Creator offers hundreds of electronic cards and also paper cards to print and color. In the Crayola Store, you can buy supplies and kits, and the Activity Book has pages you can print and color.

Figure 4.27
Crayola promotes "the power of creativity" at its Web site.

I love the design of this site—it's whimsical and functional at the same time. The backgrounds are made up of wonderful crayon artwork. There is an extensive area for teachers with lesson plans, techniques, and projects, and also a parents' area. One of my favorite pages is the e-Frigerator Art™ Gallery, where you can see artwork created by kids.

Michael's Kids Club

http://www.michaels.com/online/departments/kidsclub/kids_club.htm

The Kids Club of the Michael's Arts and Crafts Store Web site (see Figure 4.28) contains links to books and craft kits for kids. Some of the more interesting activities include making up coloring-book images and interactive jigsaw puzzles.

Figure 4.28
The home page for
Michael's Kids Club.

You can find more links on the companion Web site, or use your search engine to look for "kids" and "crafts."

5

Copyright Issues

Please note that I am not a lawyer, nor an expert on copyright. The content of this chapter has been compiled from many sources and is for your information only. Please consult with a lawyer if you have any legal questions about copyright law.

Copyright Basics

Copyright laws provide protection to creators of original works, including literary, dramatic, musical, and artistic works. According to these laws, the owner of the copyright is the only one who has the right to, among other things, distribute or reproduce these works.

Copyright law has existed since the 18th century and is even mentioned in the U.S. Constitution. It was initially created to protect written works, but over the years the law has evolved to include dramatic, musical, architectural, choreographic, pictorial, graphic, audiovisual, and other creations. The law evolves as new forms of expression are developed.

One of the most-often asked questions about copyright is whether it is necessary to register a work. You do not have to officially register your work in order for it to be protected. Protection is implicit as soon as the work is created, even if you don't put the copyright symbol on it. However, if you have to defend your copyright in court, it helps to have it registered.

The U.S. Copyright Office explains why it helps to register a work on its Web site, **http://www.loc.gov/copyright/circs/circ1.html.**

▶ Registration establishes a public record of the copyright claim.

▶ Before an infringement suit may be filed in court, registration is necessary for works of U.S. origin.

▶ If made before or within 5 years of publication, registration will establish prima facie evidence in court of the validity of the copyright and of the facts stated in the certificate.

▶ If registration is made within 3 months after publication of the work or prior to an infringement of the work, statutory damages and attorney's fees will be available to the copyright owner in court actions. Otherwise, only an award of actual damages and profits is available to the copyright owner.

Section II Researching Online

▶ Registration allows the owner of the copyright to record the registration with the U. S. Customs Service for protection against the importation of infringing copies. For additional information, request Publication No. 563, "How to Protect Your Intellectual Property Right," from: U.S. Customs Service, P.O. Box 7404, Washington, D.C. 20044. See the U.S. Customs Service Web site at **www.customs.gov** for online publications.

Registration may be made at any time within the life of the copyright, but it is no longer necessary to reregister an unpublished work if it becomes published.

If you want to protect your work by registering it for copyright, you can find the appropriate forms on the Internet at **http://www.loc.gov/copyright/reg.html**. The form includes detailed instructions.

One of the possible exceptions to copyright protection is the notion of "fair use." (Canadian copyright law has a similar concept called "fair dealing.") It is possible to quote a small portion of a protected work for the purpose of review, criticism, news reporting, or research, without necessarily violating copyright. When using copyrighted material in this way, you must include the source and the author's name.

Note that the copyright owner is not necessarily the author. In the case of work for hire, the copyright owner might end up being the person who paid for the work, rather than the author of the work. This is usually spelled out in the contract between these two parties.

For general information about the rules governing copyright and information about registration, you can visit these Web sites:

United States Copyright Office
http://www.loc.gov/copyright/ (see Figure 5.1)

Figure 5.1
The home page of the United States Copyright Office.

Canadian Intellectual Property Office
http://cipo.gc.ca/ (see Figure 5.2)

Figure 5.2
The home page of the
Canadian Intellectual
Property Office.

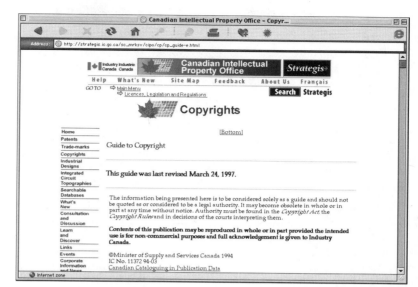

A great article about art and U.S. copyright law can be found on the Jansen Art Studio Web site. Go to **http://jansenartstudio.com/Title17.html**. David Jansen, with the assistance of the Law Department of Cornell University, wrote a lengthy article interpreting U.S. Code Title 17 (Copyrights) as it applies to decorative painting. Most of this can be applied to other crafts as well.

The Yarn Tree Web site at **http://yarntree.com/** has a similar article discussing needlecraft patterns.

Copyright on the Internet

The same copyright law that applies to the craft books you read also applies to the Internet. For example, many Web sites offer "free" projects. So what does this mean exactly?

A project usually consists of a picture, a set of instructions, perhaps a chart or an image for you to trace. This is what you get to use for free. However, this doesn't mean you are free to do whatever you want with this project. Think of it this way: What you are getting is not the project itself, but rather the permission to use the project instructions, subject to certain limitations. You need to check the fine print to find out what those limitations are. They are likely to be similar to the restrictions on what you can do with projects in craft books.

The limitations may be different from one project to another. Here are some examples of the most likely ones:

- ▶ You can't reproduce copies of the project and sell them.
- ▶ You can't turn this project into a kit and sell it.
- ▶ You can make the item for yourself only, or perhaps in small quantities for craft shows, but mass production is not allowed. For example, some projects will say that you can make up to fifty items. Other projects will not put in a number but will state that you can make as many as you want as long as they are all made by you, by hand.

Different sites may have different rules, so always be cautious and check. If this information is not readily available on the Web site, there will usually be an e-mail address you can use to request information. When in doubt, ask. If you can't find the information, you can't make any assumptions, so you should make items for your own personal use only.

Whenever you visit any Web site, be aware that everything you see is protected by copyright. For example, you can't "borrow" a graphic from a Web page and use it on your own Web page—this is stealing.The person who created that graphic has the right to determine where it is used and by whom.

There are various rules that govern discussion groups, including copyright rules. In whatever service you use, look for the "Terms of Service," where these rules are spelled out. In particular, e-mail messages and postings to public discussion lists are the property of the person who wrote them, and you cannot reproduce them without permission.

Charted needlework such as needlepoint and cross-stitch is probably the area where the most copyright violations occur on the Internet. People scan the charts and then "share" them with others. Some people are not aware of the law and do it out of ignorance. Make no mistake, though—this is stealing. If anyone asks you, "Do you share?" just say no—and mean it. You can be sued if you use someone else's work improperly.

According to an article published August 3, 2000, on cnn.com, several groups of stitchers on the Web started "sharing" patterns. As these groups grew, sales at needlework shops started to fall. This hurts designers, shop owners, and, ultimately, the crafters that they serve.

As a designer (or copyright owner), if you have evidence that your copyright has been violated, you can file a civil lawsuit in Federal district court. Unfortunately, this can be quite expensive.

Why Care About Copyrights in Crafts?
by Susan Brandt

The Hobby Industry Association (HIA) is an international trade organization of 4,000 craft & hobby companies. Its major services to members include programs of professional development, publications, tracking of issues of national concern, and promotion of the industry. HIA is the advocate for the craft & hobby industry, promoting research and information that expands awareness of the industry and its products. One area of concern to all industry members is the growing misuse of copyrighted designs and products. As more people turn to the Internet to source and share information about crafting, the lines of ownership and fair usage have begun to blur. Craft & hobby industry members became concerned about an increase in the misuse of copyrighted craft designs and products around the same time the music industry began its fight against Web sites that provided free downloads of copyrighted musical works. Understandably, any industry based on creativity has a wealth of intellectual property it wishes to protect. HIA believes that the majority of copyright infringement cases reflect a lack of knowledge of the copyright laws. So, the association is responding with an industry education program that addresses the fair usage of craft information. HIA will be providing information and tools that will help members protect their own works.

In the craft industry, designs are generally owned by the designer/creator. If it was a work for hire, another party—such as a publisher, retailer or manufacturer—will own it. An idea becomes copyrighted as soon as you put it down on paper. To determine who owns the material, look for a source name or a copyright notice that indicates the year a particular company claimed ownership of the work.

It is up to the owner to determine how the copyrighted material may be used. In almost every case, craft project designs are offered for personal use by the craft hobbyist. One example of this is the free project sheet. Project sheets are distributed with the understanding that the craft consumer is going to make that item for personal use or as a gift. The design may be free, but unless the site or printed document officially states that product is free for any use, the craft cannot be reproduced in quantities for resale. In other words, you can use a published design to make a cross-stitch sampler for your daughter or grandmother, but you can't make 100 of that design to sell to a department store.

When someone buys a craft magazine or book, the publisher or author owns the copyright to those projects. By buying a book, the consumer licenses the right to reproduce those products for individual use. Thus, it is illegal to photocopy the book to give to a friend or scan the publication for posting online. Just as you buy computer software for your own personal use and are not permitted to share copies with others, so it goes with craft books.

Granted, the entire craft industry is predicated on inspiring crafters with original designs. The issue under discussion is fair usage. Designers deserve fair pay for their creative works, and manufacturers deserve a profit for manufacturing the product and making it available. When a customer pays for a book or pattern, they are paying the designer and printer for use of that information.

To expand awareness of their products, copyright owners also license their image and information to other companies. For example, Disney® characters appear in needlework kits or fabric prints. In this case, the manufacturer of the kit or fabric pays a royalty to the licensor. Those agreements extend usage to a particular product category and are monitored carefully by the licensor for proper usage. As a consumer buying the licensed product, you may be once-removed from the licensing process but still required to adhere to copyright laws. Most large holders of well-known names and artworks are cracking down on infringers—even if you do this innocently, you can be held liable.

If you aren't sure about how a product or design can be used, there's a simple solution—ask the publisher, manufacturer, or designer if it is okay to use the design or product the way you want to use it. Copyright holders will tell you what you can and cannot do, and they can permit you to use the information or enter into a written permission agreement with you. If you are still in doubt, you may want to consult an attorney who specializes in the area of copyright and patent law.

Craft designers, learn early how to protect yourself! Put a copyright notice on every project as soon as you create it. The most basic notice includes the copyright symbol (©), year, your name, and "all rights reserved." Some companies and individuals are putting more stringent notices in the order of "reproduction of this work electronically or in print is strictly prohibited and will be prosecuted to the fullest extent of the law."

Without the creativity of designers and project manufacturers, the craft & hobby industry would have few resources to inspire consumers to discover the pleasures of crafts. Industry supporters have been helpful in getting illegal Web sites shut down, and the self-monitoring done by members of chat rooms has helped educate users. HIA will continue the awareness campaign as long as this problem persists.

Susan Brandt is HIA assistant executive director/director of communications. The HIA Web sites are:
  http://hobby.org/
  http://www.i-craft.com/

Section III
Connecting Online

"Without a sense of caring, there can be no sense of community."

—Anthony J. D'Angelo

6

Discussion Lists and Chats

Crafters are a generous bunch of people. They love to get together in groups or clubs, exchange ideas and tips, learn from each other, and simply spend time with people who enjoy the same crafts.

On the Internet, groups are formed with members all over the world. If your craft is a rare or obscure one, you might not be able to find any fellow crafters in your community, but odds are you can find kindred spirits on the Internet.

Discussion Lists

Earlier, I talked about the Internet as a tool for making connections. Nowhere is this more apparent than in discussion lists, which are a way for people with similar interests all over the world to interact and exchange information.

NOTE

A note on terminology: There are two types of online discussions—the mailing list (e-mail based) and the discussion forum (Web based). I will use the term "discussion list" to refer to all discussions.

Mailing lists are also sometimes referred to as e-mail lists or loops. Web-based discussion forums are also called message boards, bulletin boards, discussion boards, or simply forums.

Mailing Lists

A mailing list consists of a group of people who have joined together to discuss a particular topic by e-mail. You participate by sending a message to a special e-mail address for the list; your message is automatically sent to all the members of the list. Someone may reply to your message, and this person's message is sent to everyone on the list. You can then reply to their message, and so on.

Section III Connecting Online

Most mailing lists have an option called "digest." Because some mailing lists can generate a lot of e-mail, even more than one hundred messages per day, your electronic mailbox can fill up with these messages. When you use the digest option, instead of receiving all those separate messages, you get one e-mail per day containing all the messages sent to the list for that day.

You can find a searchable directory of thousands of mailing lists on the L-Soft Web site at **http://www.lsoft.com/lists/listref.html/**.

Discussion Forums

Many Web sites offer discussion forums as part of their service. For example, go to Crafter's Community at **http://crafterscommunity.com/** and click **Craft Forum** (see Figure 6.1).

Figure 6.1
Crafter's Community has a forum where members can discuss craft-related topics.

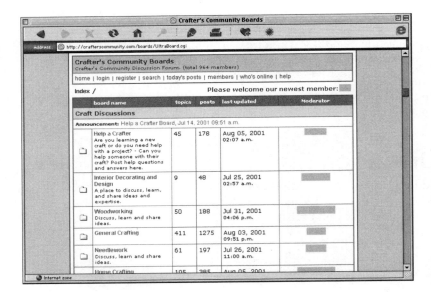

NOTE
In the Figures in this section, I have blanked out the participants' names to protect their privacy.

Figure 6.2 shows the list of topics currently under discussion and the number of messages in each topic.

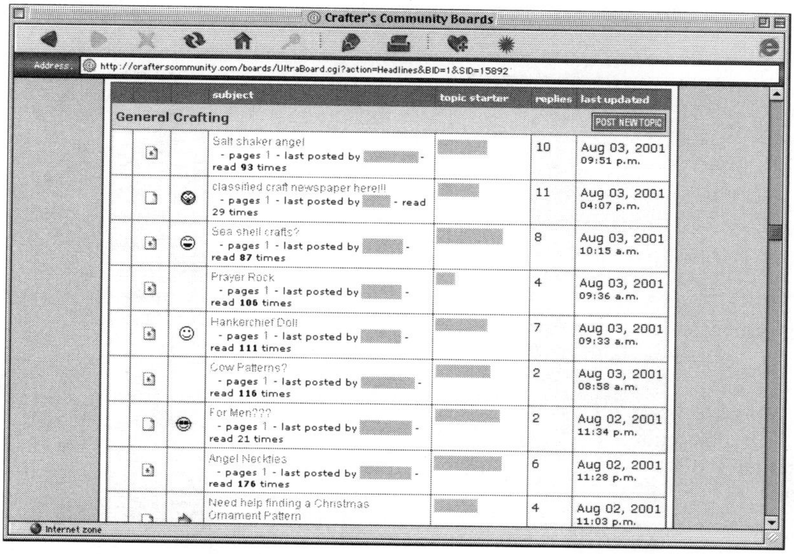

Figure 6.2
Crafter's Community
General Crafting
discussion.

If I click a topic, for example, **Sea shell crafts**, I can read all the messages in that topic (see
Figure 6.3). The first message is often a question that starts a discussion going.

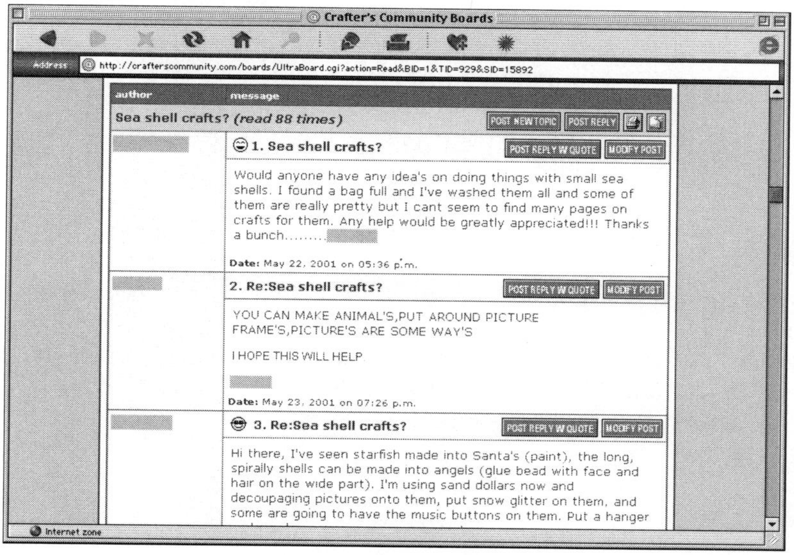

Figure 6.3
Crafter's Community
discussion on sea
shell crafts.

Section III Connecting Online

If you want to participate in the discussion, you can click the **Post Reply** button and type in your message.

In some discussion forums, anyone can read the messages, but you have to be a registered member to post messages. In others, you must register before you can get into the forum at all. Registration usually involves giving your name, sometimes a nickname you want to use, and your e-mail address. If you don't want to use your personal e-mail address, you can get one of those free e-mail accounts we talked about in Chapter 1 and use that e-mail address in discussion forums.

Another example is the Yahoo!Groups Web site at **http://groups.yahoo.com/** (see Figure 6.4), which is a leading provider of discussion forums.

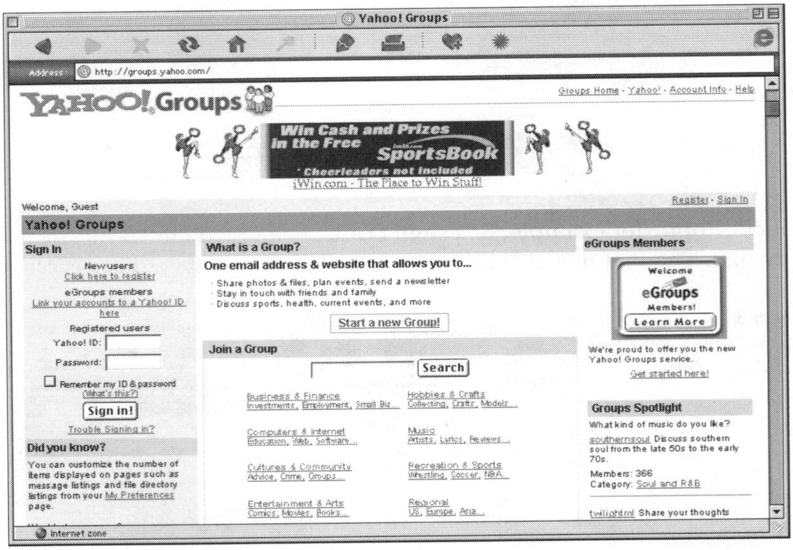

Figure 6.4
Yahoo!Groups offers access to thousands of special-interest discussion forums.

Anyone can start a list on any topic. There are thousands of lists already on Yahoo!Groups, and chances are you can find one or more that interest you. If not, just go ahead and start your own. Figure 6.5 shows the page for lists related to hobbies and crafts. The number next to each category is the number of lists, so you can see there are thousands of lists in this category alone.

Discussion Lists and Chats – Chapter 6 83

Figure 6.5
The Yahoo!Groups
Hobbies & Crafts
category.

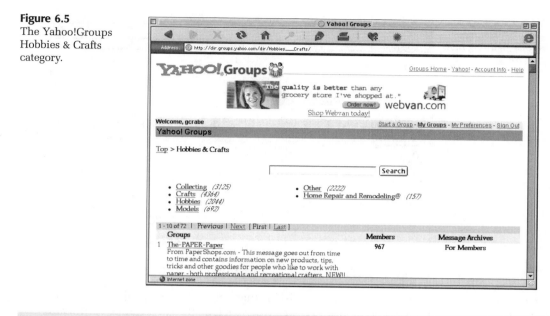

TIP

When you first join a discussion list, sit back and just read the messages for a few days so you can familiarize yourself with the tone of the list and see what people are talking about. When you feel you are ready to participate, start by posting a short message introducing yourself.

In Chapter 1, I mentioned that I subscribe to Donna Dewberry's One-Stroke mailing list (see Figure 6.6). There are currently around 1,400 people on the list who generate between fifty and one hundred messages per day. It's a wonderful place to meet other artists and to learn; there are many One-Stroke Certified Instructors who participate on the list and are happy to answer your questions.

Section III Connecting Online

http://www.muskalipman.com

Figure 6.6
The Yahoo!Groups
onestroke_painting List.

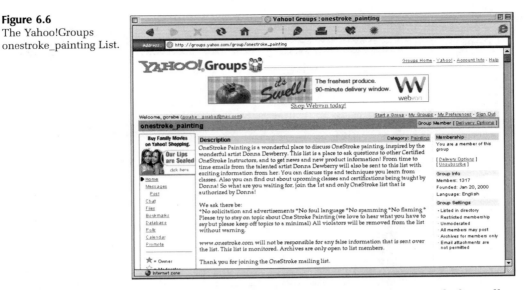

One of the things I enjoy the most about these lists is that I get to "meet" people from all over the world. A few months ago, I attended Donna Dewberry's One Stroke teaching certification class. Several of us who attended the class started our own discussion forum just so we could get to know each other, make arrangements to meet before the class, and otherwise prepare for the experience of learning and meeting each other. This list has continued after the class ended because of the friendships that were formed.

There are other sites that offer discussion forums, but the principles under which they operate are similar. In Yahoo!Groups, you can not only hold discussions but also share files. For example, on the ToleFriends list for decorative painters, participants upload pictures of their work to share with the group. Unlike other forums, all Yahoo!Groups discussion forums also operate as mailing lists, so you can choose how you want to interact with the list—on the Web or by e-mail.

You'll find discussion forums on many of the crafting Web sites (check the companion Web site). There are also other providers of forums like Topica at **http://www.topica.com/**.

Threads

So, how do these lists work, anyway?

Imagine an old-fashioned bulletin board on a wall in a public place. I put up a message that says, "Does anyone know where to find a cross-stitch pattern of a dragon?" When I come back the next day, a couple of people have posted answers to my question. Meanwhile, other people have posted questions; if I can, I post some answers, maybe post another question, and so on. After a couple of weeks, depending on how many people are checking the bulletin board, there may be dozens of messages on a variety of topics.

An electronic discussion list works the same way. In fact, it is because of this analogy that lists are still sometimes called "bulletin boards" and messages are often referred to as "posts." The difference is that messages are posted either by e-mail or on a Web site.

Let's look at an example. Say I post this question on one of my discussion lists:

> From: Geneviève
> Date: 9 March, 2001, 10:00am
> Subject: Color Theory
>
> Does anyone have some good references on color theory?

I return the next day to find two replies to my question.

> From: Sharon
> Date: 9 March, 2001, 1:15pm
> Subject: Re: Color Theory
>
> Geneviève wrote:
> > Does anyone have some good references on color theory?
>
> Jo Sonja Jansen's Color Workbook is very comprehensive and includes worksheets for you to make your own color wheel and color swatches. You might also want to check out Ann Kingslan's Guide to Mixing & Using Colour.
>
> Hope this helps,
> Sharon

The lines that start with ">" are the usual way to quote from the message to which you are replying. Because there are many threads going at once, people reading these messages might have forgotten what the question was, so the person replying includes a portion of the original message.

> From: Jackie
> Date: 9 March, 2001, 2:05pm
> Subject: Re: Color Theory
>
> Geneviève wrote:
> > Does anyone have some good references on color theory?
>
> Hi Geneviève
> My favorite book on color theory is Color Harmony Workbook:
> A Workbook and Guide to Creative Color Combinations.
>
> Jackie

Now, I ask another question.

> From: Geneviève
> Date: 10 March, 2001, 9:10am
> Subject: Dragons
>
> I'm looking to buy a dragon cross-stitch pattern. Can anyone help?
>
> Geneviève

After a while, I get an answer to this question.

> From: Anne
> Date: 10 March, 2001, 9:50am
> Subject: Re: Dragons
>
> Geneviève wrote:
> >I'm looking to buy a dragon cross-stitch pattern. Can anyone help?

Section III Connecting Online

Hi Geneviève,

I love dragons. Jennifer Aikman-Smith has some nice patterns.
Her Web site is http://www.DragonDreams.accra.ca/.

Meanwhile, there are still answers coming to the first question.

From: Ronit
Date: 10 March, 2001, 1:00pm
Subject: Re: Color Theory

Jackie wrote:
> Geneviève wrote:
> > Does anyone have some good references on color theory?

> Hi Geneviève
> My favorite book on color theory is "Color Harmony Workbook:
> A Workbook and Guide to Creative Color Combinations".

I like that book, too. You might also be interested in the
Color Matters Web site: http://www.colormatters.com/
entercolormatters.html/.

Ronit

And then another answer to the Dragon question.

From: Ronit
Date: 10 March, 2001, 1:05pm
Subject: Re: Dragons

Check also Purple Heart: http://www.purpleheart.co.uk/.
They have a lot of dragon patterns.

Ronit

Unless you've opted to receive mailing list posts in "digest" form, each message comes in a separate e-mail message in your Inbox, and you will have to sort them out. Some e-mail programs may have some features that will assist you in handling mailing lists.

If you were looking at the list of messages on a Web site forum, you would see something like this (you can follow the threads by the Subject):

Subject	From	Date
Color Theory	Geneviève	9 March, 2001, 10:00am
Re: Color Theory	Sharon	9 March, 2001, 1:15pm
Re: Color Theory	Jackie	9 March, 2001, 2:05pm
Dragons	Geneviève	10 March, 2001, 9:10am
Re: Dragons	Anne	10 March, 2001, 9:50am
Re: Color Theory	Ronit	10 March, 2001, 1:00pm
Re: Dragons	Ronit	10 March, 2001, 1:05pm

Now, this is a small example. In a list with hundreds of members, there will be a lot of threads going at the same time, with the message interspersed. It takes some getting used to, but you'll find that, with a little practice, you'll get used to following the threads that interest you. Note that different forums will have their own way of displaying messages. As we saw earlier, the Crafter's Community forums put all the messages related to the same topic together. On Yahoo!Groups, when you are viewing messages, you can choose to have them grouped by thread or listed chronologically.

Here are a few tips that will help you:

▶ Get involved. Don't be afraid to ask questions; other people probably have the same questions you have. When someone asks a question to which you know the answer, don't be shy. Discussion lists are all about sharing.

▶ Change the Subject line as required. You can see in the example above how important the Subject line of your message can be. Sometimes, in the flow of discussion, the subject matter changes; when it does, change the Subject line of the message so that people can easily scan through the messages and read what interests them.

▶ Reply privately when appropriate. Sometimes, someone will post a message, and there will follow a flurry of "me, too" or "that's great" messages. It's okay to acknowledge a message, but send a private e-mail message rather than adding another "me, too" post to the list.

Rules of Behavior

When you first join a mailing list or discussion forum, you will usually receive an e-mail message explaining the rules of the list. Read this document carefully and follow the rules as best you can. In particular, lists with a large number of members have to be stricter about their rules, because things can get out of hand more quickly.

TIP

If you join a discussion list, you will have to get used to some abbreviations and symbols that people often use to both avoid extra typing and convey emotion. Here are a few of the most common (to understand the first three, turn the book 90 degrees clockwise):

:-)	smile
;-)	wink
:-(	frown (or sad)
\<G>	grin
\<VBG>	very big grin
BTW	by the way
FWIW	for what it's worth
IMHO	in my humble opinion
LOL	laughing out loud
OTOH	on the other hand
ROTFL	rolling on the floor laughing
TTYL	talk to you later

Section III Connecting Online

Here are some important things to remember:

▶ **Stay on topic**. Different lists have different approaches to this. In a list with a small number of participants, the conversation can be casual, even if it veers off topic. In large lists, though, the rules are often more strict about staying on topic. It's okay for someone to post about a special event such as, for example, the birth of a child or a grandchild, but if too many people offer their congratulations and then follow-up with stories of their own children and so on, this can quickly take over the list.

▶ **No flaming.** Flaming refers to rude and insulting behavior that is, unfortunately, very common on the Internet. Most mailing lists do not tolerate this kind of behavior, and offenders can be banned from the list. Fortunately, crafters seem like a pretty easygoing bunch, and I have never seen any incidents of flaming on any of the crafting lists in which I participate.

▶ **No soliciting or advertising.** This rule varies from one list to another, but usually it is considered bad form to take advantage of a mailing list for blatant advertising, except on lists that are set up for this purpose.

▶ **Do not misuse the list of members.** This follows from the previous point. Some people will sign on to a mailing list just long enough to harvest the list of members to use for mass advertising. This practice is severely frowned upon.

Also remember that a discussion list is a public place. Don't say anything in an online discussion that you wouldn't want the whole world to see.

Don't let all the rules discourage you; they are mainly based on common sense, anyway. The bottom line is to enjoy yourself. You will meet people from all over the world with whom you share interests, and I promise you will have a great time.

Start Your Own Discussion List

In Yahoo!Groups, and other similar services, you can create your own discussion list; Yahoo!Groups is an especially good option because a group can be accessed either as a mailing list or as a Web-based discussion forum. Whether it's for a small or large group, the process is very simple. Figure 6.7 shows the beginning of the form you have to fill out; you just provide all the information needed, like the name of your list (or group), what category it should go in, etc.

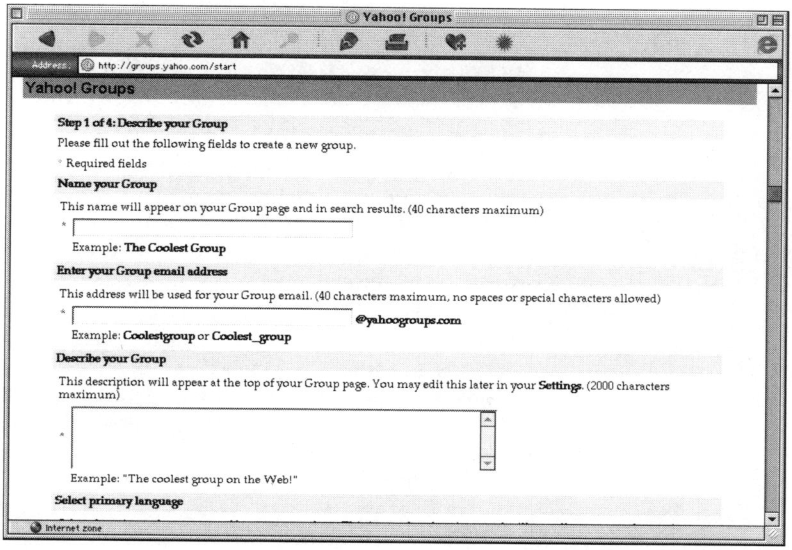

Figure 6.7
Form to Create
a New Group.

You have various options for people joining the list. You can leave that completely open so that anyone can join at any time, or you can have people request to join subject to your approval.

The group itself can be publicly available, or you can make it unlisted if it's a private list, for example a list for a local group that meets in person periodically and corresponds through the mailing list the rest of the time.

Finally, you can create a list to which only you can post messages. Why would you want to do that? You could use this feature to publish an e-mail newsletter. People would subscribe to your newsletter by joining the mailing list, and you publish your newsletter by sending it to the group. You don't have to worry about managing a large mailing list—it's all taken care of for you.

Topica, at **http://www.topica.com/**, is another service where you can create your own discussion forums.

ToleFriends is one of the Yahoo!Groups lists to which I belong. It includes amateur and professional tole painters, teachers, and award winners. Anne Strebe started this list in November, 2000, and I asked her some questions about discussion lists.

Section III Connecting Online

INTERVIEW   An Interview with Anne Strebe

Anne Strebe runs the ToleFriends list on Yahoo!Groups from her home in
Venezuela. This is quite a large list with more than 1,200 members.
Discussion is lively, generating on average one hundred messages per day.

Q: How long have you been participating in online discussion groups?

Our town got connected to the Internet in August, 1997. I found the ToleNet
Web site and a few days later joined their mailing list.

Since then I participated with ToleNet, appreciating the information and help
I was able to get through the mailing list and giving back whenever this was
possible for me.

I did tentatively join other mailing lists on the (Inter)Net after joining ToleNet.
But, as I like to participate actively and time would not allow me to do this
with equal frequency on several lists, I decided to reduce my participation to
just one list. This does not mean that in my opinion other lists are less
informative or would not be equally interesting for any painter. This is more a
personal decision; it's normally in my nature not to diversify too much.

Q. What is ToleFriends about?

ToleFriends is a free mailing list with open membership and not moderated.
It was started the day after ToleNet had to interrupt their mailing list due to
technical problems.

I live in South America, in a small industrial town in the south of Venezuela.
Decorative painting is still not well known in our country, as quality supplies
are practically not available. In our region, decorative painting is still
considered a hobby for crafters and housewives who are bored.

When I had access to the Internet and joined a mailing list, I was stunned by
the wealth of information available to me and freely given on mailing lists.

When the ToleNet mailing list had technical difficulties and was interrupted, I
thought of the many friendships I had made through this mailing list, how sad
it would be not to have a place to continue these friendships, and started
ToleFriends.

It is primarily a painting-related mailing list, but, as the name says, friendship
is as important as tole or painting to us. It is an interactive list; painting is part
of our lives, but so are other things we would share with a friend we meet at a
coffee shop or a group meeting—things like an illness we or someone in our
family has, worries, and prayer requests.

Actually, ToleFriends is as much about friendship and reaching out to each
others as it is about tole or decorative painting.

Q. Describe the members of ToleFriends

Our membership has grown in only five months to close to 1,000; our
membership consists of a great variety of people. We are international, with
members from Japan, Australia, South America, Europe, Canada, and the
USA, though most members are from the these last two countries.

As well, the experience of our members ranges from Master Decorative Artists
(the highest classification given by the Society of Decorative Painters), holders
of the Vesterheim Gold Medal, to published authors, travel teachers, local
teachers, and beginners who only picked up a paintbrush a few weeks ago.

Everyone is welcome to join and participate or just listen in.

INTERVIEW   **An Interview with Anne Strebe (Cont.)**

Q. What sort of information is exchanged on the list?

Mainly painting-related information Such as:

- ▶ questions about supplies:
  - ▶ where to obtain these
  - ▶ sharing of special offers in certain chain stores and mail-order sources
  - ▶ color conversion
  - ▶ information about new products
- ▶ questions about certain techniques, styles, problems a lister encounters doing a project
- ▶ information about painting seminars, conventions, and setting up a meeting between listers
- ▶ requests for information and help when a problem with a painted project occurs
- ▶ sharing accomplishments with a painted project.

Listers who suffer from certain ailments that can make their painting days difficult but who, at the same time, use painting as a therapy compare their experience, speak up on the list about it, and have been able to reach out to each other.

Q. What are your future plans for the list?

On-line discussions of certain techniques and projects are planned and other new programs. As ToleFriends is only a few months old, many new things are "in the making."

ToleFriends also has its own Web site at **http://www.tolefriends.com/** (See Figure 6.8).

Figure 6.8
The ToleFriends
Web site.

Section III Connecting Online

Online Chats

You may have heard the term "chat room" or "online chat." These terms refer to a mode of communication quite different from the discussion list. Unlike discussion lists, where conversation takes place over days or weeks and each participant reads messages and replies at his or her leisure, a chat occurs in real time. All the participants are logged on at the same time; the conversation consists of text typed into a common window. Everyone sees what everyone else is typing.

Figure 6.9 shows an example of a chat window in Yahoo!Groups; each discussion list has its own chat area. In this window, I am currently the only participant. Most chats look like this; the large rectangle is where the contribution of all the participants show up; when you want to say something, you enter it in the smaller field below and click **Send**.

Figure 6.9
The Yahoo!Groups
Chat Window.

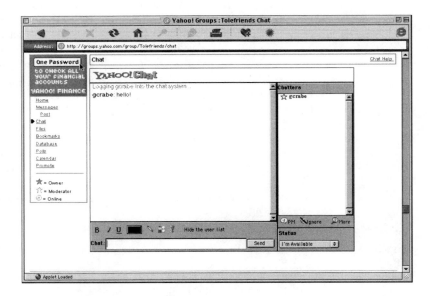

Here is an example of what you might experience in a chat room. In this chat, my name is "polarian." Some people use their own name in a chat, while others prefer to use a nickname or pseudonym to preserve their privacy.

> **polarian**: has joined the chat.
>
> **polarian**: Hi this is Geneviève
>
> **sue459**: Hi Gen
>
> **sorepaws**: Hi Geneviève
>
> **polarian**: Does anyone have any tips on sealing a papier-mâché box before painting?
>
> **ronit**: Hi Gen, long time no see!
>
> **sue459**: Have any of you painted on CDs?

sorepaws: I usually put on a coat of Gesso then basecoat.

polarian: Sue, I have heard of someone who painted on old CDs and makes wind chimes.

sue459: Gen, I don't usually seal, I just basecoat.

sorepaws: Do any of you belong to The National Society of Decorative Painters? Do you find it worthwhile?

ronit: Gen, do you know how the CDs are prepped?

sue459: SDP membership is great. Their magazine is outstanding, and if you ever have the opportunity to attend one of their conventions, don't miss it.

sorepaws: Thanks, Sue.

sue459: Does anyone know the URL for Phyllis Tilford's Web site?

Things can go pretty fast, so anything that saves typing is fair game. The special symbols and abbreviations described earlier are also used.

Now, there are only four participants in this chat. You can imagine that things can get somewhat confusing with a few dozen people. You have to be on your toes to follow all the simultaneous conversations. Some chats are set up for a specific reason and last for a short time; others are going all the time, with people popping in and out.

Some people love to chat all the time, while others find it too confusing, too fast, or too difficult to keep up. Give it a try if you get the opportunity—you may find that you enjoy it.

The "celebrity" chat can be a lot of fun. These are generally announced ahead of time and, unlike other chats, this are not a free-for-all, but rather a structured question-and-answer session. Participants ask the questions one at a time, and the celebrity answers. For example, Donna Dewberry conducts quarterly online chats for subscribers to her online magazine, The Stroking Edge. Frequently, these chats are hosted or moderated.

If you want to set up your own chat, you can use a service like TalkCity at **http://www.talkcity.com/**. Yahoo! also has a chat service at **http://chat.yahoo.com/**.

7

Online Communities

As I mentioned in the previous chapter, crafting communities have always existed, usually consisting of a group of crafters in the same neighborhood or town who get together occasionally to exchange tips or work together on joint projects. The Internet extends this concept by removing both geographical and time barriers and lets you communicate easily with people all over the world.

An online community is a particular kind of Web site that offers a variety of information and, in addition, provides discussion groups or chat areas that allow you to interact with other people. I think of the difference between a conventional Web site and an online community as the difference between a presentation and a meeting. Usually, a Web site consists of information that is presented to you; a community is like a meeting where people interact with each other.

Let's look at an example. About.com (Figure 7.1) is a large Web site made up of a collection of communities of individuals with common interests.

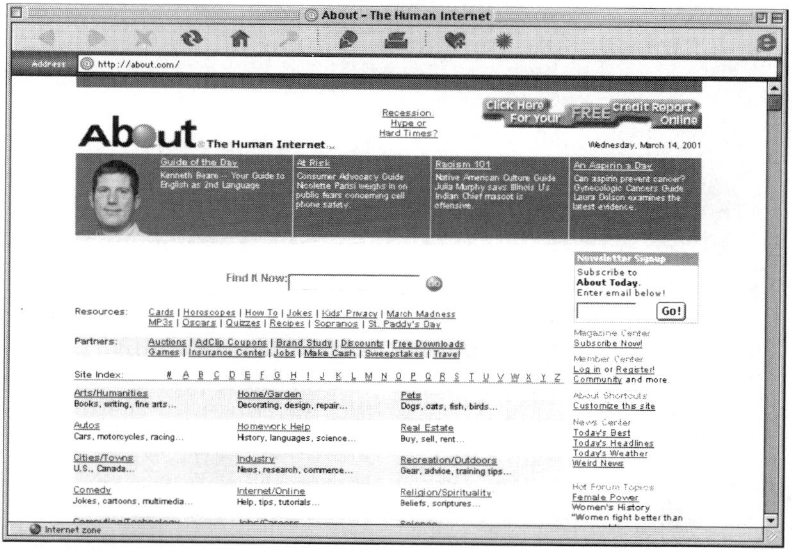

Figure 7.1
About.com lobby.

The site is made up of several hundred separate topic areas. Each area has a host who is described as a "professional guide who is carefully screened and trained by About. Guides build a comprehensive environment around each of their specific topics, including the best new content, relevant links, How-To's, Forums, and answers to just about any question" (see **http://ourstory.about.com/**). There are Web links, discussion groups, a tremendous amount of information, files to download, and more.

The hobby area (Figure 7.2) is at **http://about.com/hobbies/**. Click the name of the hobby that interests you to enter that topic area. For example, let's try Cross-Stitch. The topic area for Cross-Stitch (see Figure 7.3) contains many subjects, including Free Patterns, Designers, and Styles.

Figure 7.2
About.com Hobbies.

Figure 7.3
About.com Cross-Stitch
part 1.

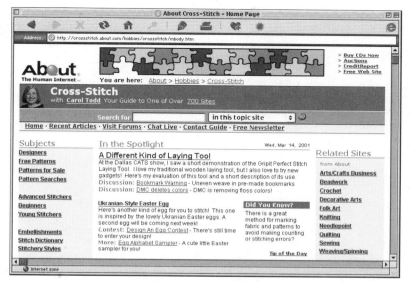

In each area, you'll find a welcome from your guide telling you a little about himself or herself. The guide in the Cross-Stitch area at the time of this writing is Carol Todd, and she expresses her thoughts about her role:

> *"Cross-stitching is my passion, and the Net is a wonderful resource for stitchers. I'll guide you to the best sites on the Net to improve your stitching, learn new techniques, find free patterns, and meet other stitchers. I also love designing, so I'll be posting lots of free charts and a new alphabet every month."*

At the top of the screen in Figure 7.3, you can see the various components that are often part of community sites. These include:

► Articles
► Forums (discussion lists)
► Live chats
► A free e-mail newsletter

Let's scroll down a bit and see what else is available (see Figure 7.4). There are free patterns, a store locator, a photo gallery of cross-stitch projects, and information for both beginning and advanced stitchers.

Section III Connecting Online

Figure 7.4
About.com Cross-Stitch
part 2.

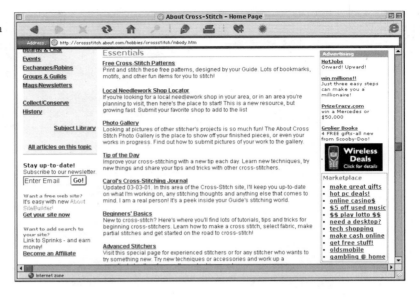

In the previous chapter, you saw how discussion lists work in Yahoo!Groups. At About.com, each topic area has discussion groups (forum or bulletin board). Figure 7.5 shows the discussions in the cross-stitch area.

Figure 7.5
About.com Cross-Stitch
Forums.

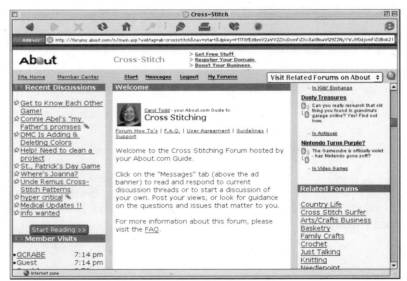

Whatever craft you are interested in, you can probably find an area in About.com that will provide you with information, Web links, and contact with other crafters.

Crafting Communities

There are many community sites that are specifically designed for crafters. I will highlight a few here, and you can find more on the companion Web site.

Craftideas

http://www.craftideas.com/

Craftideas (see Figure 7.6) is the home of some great magazines, including *Crafts 'n Things*, *Painting*, and *Cross Stitcher*. The site features free newsletters, projects, discussion groups, and contests. There are crafts for kids, crafts for beginners, and seasonal crafts. One innovative section is Craft Healthy, which contains articles on how crafting can be good for your health.

Figure 7.6
The Craftideas
home page.

INTERVIEW

An Interview with Heather Fox

Heather Fox is new media director at Clapper Communications, publisher of several craft magazines, such as Pack-O-Fun, Craft 'n Things, Painting, Cross Stitcher, *and the craftideas.com Web site.*

Q: How did the craftideas.com Web site get started?

In 1995, several sites were created for the craft magazines. These were the first craft magazines to have their own Web sites. In 2000, the various sites were consolidated under the Craftideas name.

Q: Tell me about the Craftideas community.

Crafters in general are a rather unique community. They like to talk about their crafts and are very helpful with each other. An online community is a natural extension; it is especially useful for people who live far away from other crafters, stores, etc.

Craftideas includes many community elements such as shopping, message boards, newsletters, and classified ads.

Q. I noticed you offer downloadable projects for purchase.

Many of the projects from the magazines are available to be purchased individually and downloaded from the Web site directly onto the user's computer.

There are several advantages. This is great for the professional crafter who is interested in specific projects that are great craft show sellers, especially if the back issues of the magazines are no longer available. Also, this provides greater availability to international customers of projects that might not be cost-effective to distribute in print and ship overseas.

Q: The Craft Healthy section is rather unique. What is it about?

This is an important part of our company mission. Research has shown a link between crafts and improved health, and there are several articles on this subject on the Web site.

Q: Are there areas on the site that can help crafters with research?

There are three sections that would be especially helpful:

▶ The Craft Professor, for someone wanting to learn the basics of a new craft.

▶ Craft Trends, research on trends that can help crafters predict what will sell at craft shows.

▶ Ask the Experts, which provides answers to readers' crafting questions.

Q: What do you see in the future for craftideas.com?

We will be expanding the magazine sites, adding more downloadable projects, and publishing online-only issues of the magazines. We plan to add more niche items—items that may not be cost-effective to distribute in print but can be distributed electronically via e-mail, CD-ROMs, and the Web.

CraftersCommunity.com
http://www.crafterscommunity.com

The Crafter's Community site (see Figure 7.7) has discussion forums, a chat room, and hundreds of craft links. In addition, there is a Craft Supply Swap, where you can trade or sell your unwanted craft supplies, and a Craft Project Swap, where crafters can set up groups for the purpose of exchanging handmade crafts with other crafters.

Figure 7.7
The Crafter's
Community
home page.

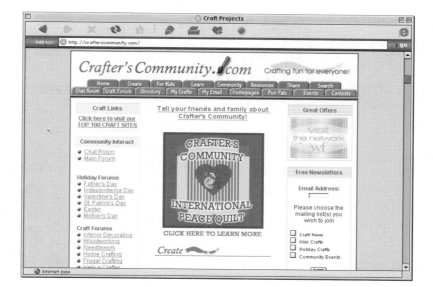

Section III Connecting Online

CraftPlanet

http://www.craftplanet.com/

CraftPlanet (see Figure 7.8) is an eclectic site that offers some of the usual features like discussion groups and free projects, but it also includes articles on inspiration and creativity, success stories, and a special section for teachers.

Figure 7.8
The CraftPlanet
home page.

Sharing Images

When you are participating in online communities, one of the things you want to be able to do is share pictures of your crafts.

The first thing you need to do is capture pictures of your crafts and get them into your computer. There are several ways to do this, using a conventional camera and a scanner or a digital camera. I touched a bit on this in Chapter 1 and will explain it in more detail in Chapter 13. Once you have captured an image, you want to save it in a format called JPEG or JPG. Without getting into all the technical details, this is the most appropriate format for displaying photographs online.

Next, you need to find a place on the Web where you can display these pictures for your friends to see. There are many such places. One of them is PhotoPoint at **http://www.photopoint.com/** (see Figure 7.9). You can use this site to store, organize, and share your pictures and even order prints. There are other similar sites out there (see the companion Web site for links). Their procedures will not be identical, but the steps will be similar.

Figure 7.9
The PhotoPoint
home page.

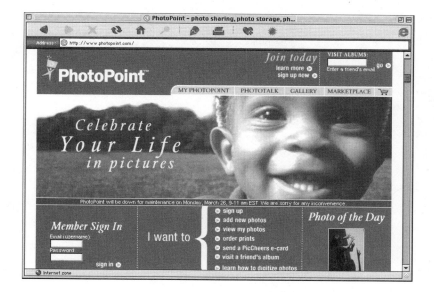

For the purposes of this book, I set up an album on PhotoPoint so I could see for myself (and for you) how easy the process is. I found that the online instructions were pretty easy to follow. First, I had to set up an account; this involved filling in a form with my name, e-mail address, and so on. Once I had done that, I received an e-mail with my password. The next step was to sign in and upload some pictures.

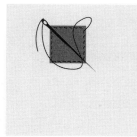

TIP

You have probably heard the words "upload" and "download." These refer to copying a file (this could be a document, a picture, a movie file, etc.) from one computer to another. "Downloading" refers to copying a file from another computer or Web site to your computer; "uploading" is the opposite, copying a file from your computer to another computer or Web site. In the case of PhotoPoint, we are uploading pictures from my computer to the PhotoPoint Web site.

I clicked **My PhotoPoint**, signed in, and then clicked **add new photos** which took me to the screen in Figure 7.10.

Figure 7.10
PhotoPoint—
Adding Pictures.

Choose how many pictures you want to upload (I chose three). Click the **Browse** button for each picture you want to upload. You then navigate through your hard disk and locate the picture file. Once you have selected your pictures, click the **Add photos now** button and your photos will be uploaded to the site.

You can then go to your Photo Inbox and see the pictures you have uploaded (see Figure 7.11).

Figure 7.11
PhotoPoint—
Photo Inbox.

Finally, you can move pictures from the Inbox to an album (see Figure 7.12). You can have several albums; some can be shared, which means that anyone who has your e-mail address can see them, or you can have some albums protected by a password so that only people to whom you have given the password can see the album.

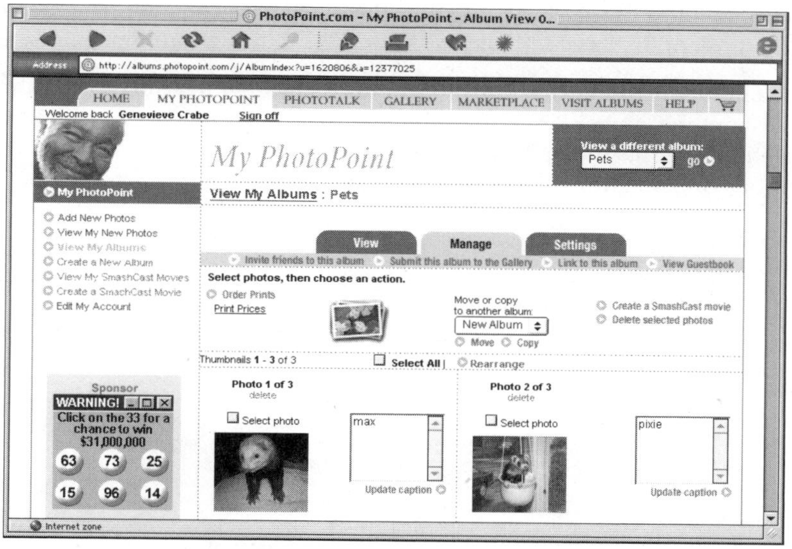

Figure 7.12
PhotoPoint—Album
Management.

If you click **Link to this album**, you will get the Web link that you can send your friends so they can view your album. When they visit, they will see something like Figure 7.13.

Figure 7.13
PhotoPoint—
Viewing Album.

In addition to storing photographs of your crafts, you can also use PhotoPoint to share scrapbook pages that you can scan into your computer with a scanner. You can find URLs of other similar services on the companion Web site.

Section III Connecting Online

Subscribing to Newsletters

Another way to keep up with what is going on in the crafting world is subscribing to online newsletters. Most of the sites I mentioned earlier in this chapter have free newsletters, usually weekly or monthly, to which you can subscribe simply by giving your e-mail address.

For example, each topic area in About.com has its own newsletter. In Yahoo!Groups, which we talked about in Chapter 6, many people use the discussion list mechanism to send out newsletters. On the Topica Web site at **http://www.topica.com/** (see Figure 7.14), there are thousands of free newsletters for you to choose from.

Figure 7.14

The Topica home page invites you to subscribe to a newsletter—or start your own.

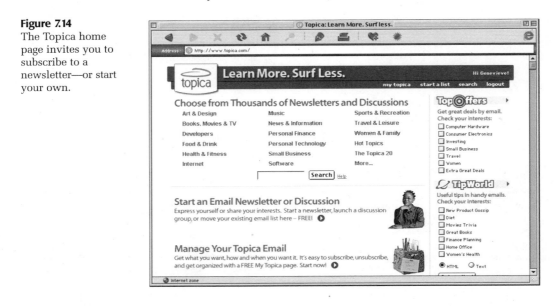

TIP

When you subscribe to a newsletter, you will receive a welcome message via e-mail. Be sure to save this message; it contains the instructions on how to unsubscribe from the newsletter, which you may need some day.

Many commercial craft supply sites also have newsletters, which are usually a combination of crafting tips and information on products for sale. You'll find many supplier links on the companion Web site.

Your Privacy and Your Rights

Whether you are participating in a discussion on a community site, subscribing to a newsletter, or sharing pictures on a site like PhotoPoint, you need to be aware of your rights. There are two things you need to check: a site's privacy policy and its terms of service. Most sites will have a link to these two items on their main page (usually in very small print on the bottom of the page).

A Web site's privacy policy should spell out, among other things:

▶ What information is collected about you

▶ What the owners of the site will and won't do with this information

▶ Whether they will ask your permission before releasing information to other companies for advertising purposes

▶ How your account information is protected

If there is anything in a site's privacy policy that you're not sure about or you don't understand, there will usually be a Help link or an e-mail address so you can ask questions.

If you are interested in issues of online privacy, here are some Web sites you can check out:

▶ Electronic Frontier Foundation: **http://www.eff.org/**

▶ Privacy.net: **http://www.privacy.net/**

▶ PrivacyPlace: **http://www.privacyplace.com/**

▶ PrivacyTimes: **http://www.privacytimes.com/**

For more sites, go to your favorite search engine and look for "Internet privacy."

A Web site's terms of service describe both your rights and obligations and their own. This usually includes a code of conduct for members, as well as certain rights assumed by the Web site owners over information you post to the site. This latter point is important to note. For example, on some sites where you can create photo albums, you may be giving the site owners some rights with respect to your pictures, so make sure you read and understand their terms before you upload anything.

Section III Connecting Online

8

Crafting
for Charity

*"The true meaning of life is to plant trees,
under whose shade you do not expect to sit."*

—Nelson Henderson

In the previous chapter, I talked about how crafters like to form communities. One of the things a lot of crafters enjoy doing is creating crafts for non-profit organizations. Some projects involve knitting or crocheting blankets, clothes, or toys for sick children; others involve fund-raising by selling finished craft objects.

The Internet provides new ways to publicize programs, keep crafters in touch with each other, and give a much wider scope to some very worthwhile projects.

Connect with Charitable Projects

If you participate in an online discussion list for your particular craft, just ask and you may find out that some of the people on the list are already involved in a charitable project. If not, here are a few examples of places on the Web where you can start your search.

Charity Crafts, at **http://www.thefamily.com/countrycottage/charity/** (see Figure 8.1), contains links to various projects that involve crochet, knitting, or sewing for charity. There are also links to sites that offer a variety of free patterns for clothes of all sizes, blankets, and other items suitable for these charitable projects.

Section III Connecting Online

Figure 8.1
Charity Crafts is a resource for those who want to sew, crochet, or knit for charity.

The site also includes free patterns for various items, including:

▶ Baby caps or booties for newborn or premature infants

▶ Afghans for babies, older children, and nursing homes

▶ Caps for people undergoing chemotherapy

▶ Teddy bears and other toys

▶ Hats, mittens, and scarves

▶ Slippers and socks

▶ Wheelchair totes

Note that the patterns are free only if you use them for non-profit purposes. There is also a lot of information on the sizes required for various purposes.

If you like to crochet, the Crochet for Charities Links Web site at **http://home.inreach.com/ marthac/charity.html** (see Figure 8.2) has a collection of links that will point you to a lot of projects.

Figure 8.2
Crochet for Charities Links can point you to dozens of charities with needs.

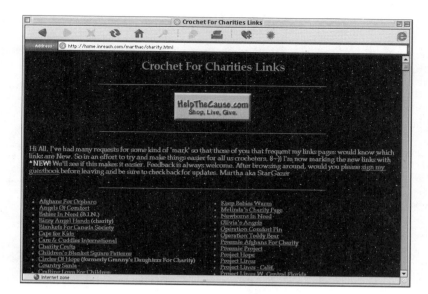

On the CraftIdeas.com Web site, in the Craft Healthy section, there are several articles on crafting for charity (see Figure 8.3), including Web links to various projects. Some articles relate success stories, and others highlight worthwhile organizations with which you might want to get involved.

Figure 8.3
Crafting for Charity on craftideas.com.

The All Crafts for Charity Web site, at **http://coingo.net/ac4c/** (see Figure 8.4), provides information on many charity projects involving sewing, crocheting, knitting, quilting, tatting, smocking, and other fabric crafts. It also has a Yahoo!Groups discussion list at **http://groups.yahoo.com/group/Allcrafts4charity/**.

Every month, the members work on "Buddy Projects," where they partner with a particular charity and create hand-made items for needy people of the world. Members of All Crafts for Charity can be found in several countries around the world.

Figure 8.4
All Crafts for Charity also focuses on stitching and fabric crafts.

INTERVIEW

I asked this question on the All Crafts for Charity (AC4C) list: I would be interested in your thoughts on how the Internet (Web sites, lists like this one, etc.) has helped these kinds of projects.

From Shell McCoy:

For me, it's been a wonderful opportunity to find out the needs of particular areas and how they differ (as well as the mutual challenges).

Moreover, it's been an integral instrument in meeting people that one would not otherwise meet because of physical barriers. On this list we have several members with physical challenges that would otherwise not be able to go to work meetings, seminars, or classes. We have been able to be enriched by their presence because of this media form. These people that are sometimes homebound are able to teach and touch everyone on this list.

There's also the cost factor. So many places charge for space for meeting rooms, materials, etc. Some national charities actually charge their volunteers for patterns. A list like this one enables us to share EVERYTHING at no charge. Members have come forward with fabric donations, materials donations, and monetary donations to other members when needed (when they could not afford postage or materials but wanted desperately to help). We don't have to charge membership fees or tithings. No money is required to do *anything* save the money spent on one's personal materials.

Most importantly, one of my greatest satisfactions (the greatest of course being to help those less fortunate) has been watching the friendships made on the list. It's a group "pen pal" list. Several members have met in real life to have picnics, luncheons, what have you. Several have offered their homes during vacation times. We all share our joys and sorrows as a loving family would.

From Beth Koskie:

I think it's done a couple of things (at least) for me. I was not connected to any local group when I joined this group, so it gave me an outlet to groups around the country who needed the skills I had to offer...also, I have learned a tremendous amount about babies, NICUs, and topics I knew nothing about when I started. Having lost a nephew from SIDS, I still knew little or nothing about the variety of losses and near-losses families experience, as well as not knowing that there really could be babies going home in this country wrapped in newspapers because families had *nothing* for them! In addition, I've formed some wonderful friendships with the women on this list, and I love being part of their lives and having them as part of mine. There is a bonding that happens when we join in a common cause to help babies and their families...and we develop an appreciation for the variety of skills we all bring to the table.

Section III Connecting Online

Of course, you can make use of a lot of the free patterns available on other Web sites—just be sure you check the permissions or ask if the patterns can be used for this purpose.

Now, let me introduce you to the two projects with which I am involved.

The Memory Box Program

I learned of the Memory Box program through some online friends on the ToleFriends mailing list. I joined the program just a few months ago, and it has become a very rewarding part of my life.

The Memory Box Program

The Memory Box program started when a group of painters realized that in hospitals, there was a need for boxes to hold keepsakes for families that lost infant children to miscarriage or early death. The boxes are a small way that we can help acknowledge the importance of the life these women carried inside of them. Through painting, we can create a keepsake box that the family may keep for generations. We think that this is a very worthy project and are proud to be a part of it.

Since our launch in June, 1998 at the National SDP (Society of Decorative Painters) convention, we have 437 painters signed up to paint or help pay for boxes, and 103 chapters of the SDP participating. As of March 27, 2001, Memory Box Artists have shipped 17,220 boxes. We need over 1300 boxes per month to support the hospitals that we have committed to in the U.S. and Canada. We have 375 hospitals in the U.S., Canada, Germany, Italy, New Zealand, Australia, and Venezuela that we have either sent or promised boxes to.

Tera Leigh and Marie Gemmil worked with members of MEND (Mommies Enduring Neonatal Death) and RESOLVE to identify hospitals with quality infant bereavement programs to guarantee that the boxes go for the purpose for which they were painted. The people who run these programs are fiercely dedicated to helping families through the devastation of losing a child. If you know of a hospital that has an infant bereavement program in place and would be interested in receiving boxes, please contact Marie with the name, address, and phone number of the hospital, and the name of the contact person for the bereavement program.

To paint for the program, contact Marie Gemmil (mgemmil@netadventure.com) for details. We provide program guidelines and information about infant loss. You may participate as much as you have time to. Even if you only paint one box, you will be helping! We have many teachers who donate class time to get their students to paint for us, as a one time event. We are grateful for every box we can get to a hospital!

The Memory Box Program has its own Web site at **http://www.teraleigh.com/memoryboxes/** (see Figure 8.5) and a mailing list at **http://groups.yahoo.com/group/memoryboxes**.

Figure 8.5
The Memory Box
Program Web site.

Project Linus

Project Linus provides knitted and crocheted blankets for children in hospitals. It has given me a way to make my television-watching time productive. I love to crochet afghans, but let's face it—I really only need so many blankets in my house. This project will give me an unlimited outlet for my crocheted blankets.

How did I find out about this project? I had heard about organizations that donate hand-made blankets, so I searched the Internet and found many worthwhile projects. I picked Project Linus at **http://www.projectlinus.org/** (see Figure 8.6) because there is a local chapter I can work with.

Figure 8.6
Project Linus
volunteers recently
donated their
300,000th blanket.

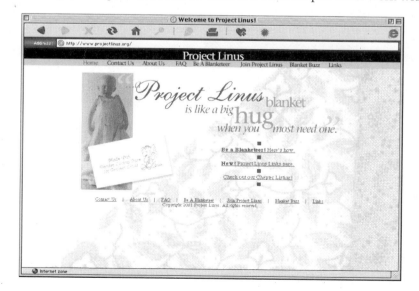

Section III Connecting Online

According to its Web site, by July 2001, Project Linus had delivered more than 300,000 security blankets to children around the world. The organization lays claim to more than 250 chapters in the United States, with affiliate chapters in Canada and England. The Web site lists contact information for all the chapters.

Fund-Raising

Crafts have always been popular as fund-raising items. We have all seen fairs with handmade items displayed to raise money for non-profit organizations.

If you are involved in such an activity, the Internet can dramatically increase the size of your audience. Selling on the Internet has been successful for many businesses, and it can be so for your fund-raising efforts as well.

In Section V, I will talk about how and what to sell online. Although that section is primarily aimed at craft businesses, there is no reason you can't use the methods described there for fund-raising. You can set up your own Web site, use existing electronic-commerce services, or even use auction sites to sell crafts. You can keep your costs very low and still advertise to a very large audience.

For example, the auction site eBay has become a very popular way for charitable organizations to raise funds by putting donated items up for auction. This is popular because eBay reaches such a large audience. You can also use online classified ads, which are available either for free or at very low cost. Look for many more ideas in Chapter 12.

You can also set up your own electronic commerce Web site (see Chapters 12 and 13). Some providers of e-commerce Web sites charge lower fees to non-profit organizations.

Section IV
Buying Online

"Efficiency is intelligent laziness."

—David Dunham

9
Online Shopping

There has been a boom in online shopping in the last few years for two main reasons: choice and convenience. While shopping online may never replace going to a store in person, the variety of merchandise available is much greater that what is available within driving distance. Online shopping is especially useful if your hobby is uncommon; you have a better chance to find scarce supplies when you have the whole Internet to search. It's also great if you live far from sources of craft supplies.

For those of you who are apprehensive about shopping on the Internet, this chapter explains how online shopping works and how to make sure your credit card number is handled safely.

How It Works

There are three steps involved in online shopping, just like shopping in a store. First, you find the items you are looking for, then you put them in your virtual shopping cart, and then you check out. The shopping cart metaphor was developed because it's something people are familiar with.

I will use the Barnes & Noble (B&N) online bookstore at **http://www.bn.com/** as an example as I explain the steps. Figure 9.1 shows the main page of the Barnes & Noble Web site.

Figure 9.1
Barnes & Noble's main page presents numerous shopping choices.

The B&N site contains several stores selling books, CDs, videos, and more. Each area functions pretty much the same way. This example will show how to order from the bookstore.

The first step is to click **Bookstore** to go to the main page of the bookstore (Figure 9.2).

Figure 9.2
The first page of
Barnes & Noble.com's
Bookstore.

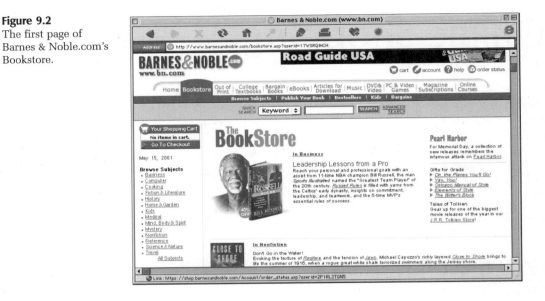

The next step is finding what you want to buy; a typical online store will have several ways of allowing you to locate products, just like a real store does. The following are most typical:

▶ Most sites will highlight new products on their main page. In the case of B&N, new releases are prominently displayed. This is like the cardboard displays you see at the front of a bookstore, showcasing major new releases.

▶ Sales and specials are also usually highlighted on a Web site's main page. This is like the sales flyer you might find in your newspaper.

▶ You can browse through the available products. On the B&N site, using the Browse Subjects links on the left is like browsing through the various sections of the bookstore. Use this feature if you're not sure what you're looking for or if you are visiting the site for the first time and you want to see what is available. This is like browsing through the aisles of a store.

▶ If you are looking for something specific, use the Search feature. This is like asking a store employee to help you locate a particular author or a particular book.

In our B&N example, let's say we want to look for books by designer Kaffe Fassett. In the search area just above the center of the window, we choose to search by **Author**, enter the name in the search box (see Figure 9.3), and click the **Search** button.

Figure 9.3
Using the Barnes &
Noble.com Author
Search function.

The next page to appear (see Figure 9.4) shows a list of books by Kaffe Fassett. You can scroll
down the page and see small pictures of the book covers and detailed information about the
book format, publisher, date of publication, and price.

Figure 9.4
An example of search
results at bn.com.

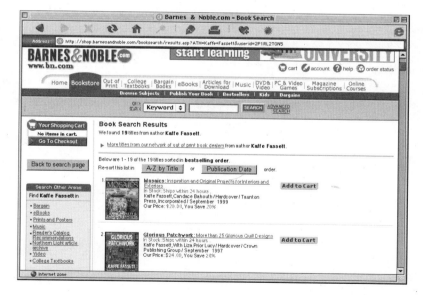

You can now pick a book of interest—say, in this case, *Mosaics*—and click the title. The next page (see Figure 9.5) shows a larger picture and more detailed information about the book.

Figure 9.5
A Barnes & Noble.com book description.

If you want to buy this book, you click the "Add to Cart" button, which will put the book in your virtual shopping cart. In Figure 9.6, on the right-hand side you can see that the book has been placed in the shopping cart.

Figure 9.6
You're on your way to making a purchase.

You can repeat this process to find more books and put them in your virtual shopping cart. When you have chosen all the items you want to order, you can look at the contents of your cart by clicking the **cart** button on the top right of the page.

The virtual shopping cart (see Figure 9.7) is represented by a Web page containing a list of the books you have selected. Once you have put all the books you want in your shopping cart, click **Go To Checkout**. Don't worry, you haven't bought anything yet—you will have several opportunities to change your mind.

Figure 9.7
The shopping cart page displays the items you wish to purchase.

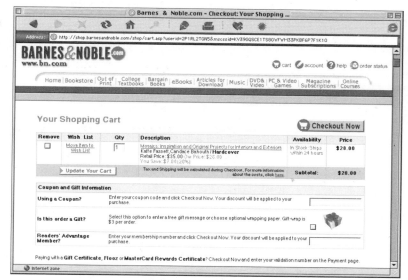

Once you proceed to the checkout (see Figure 9.8), you are asked whether you have shopped here before.

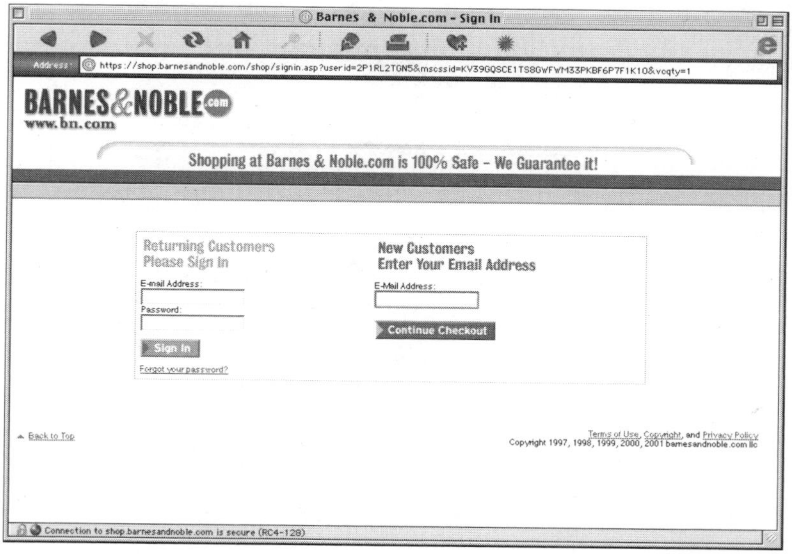

Figure 9.8
To make a purchase, you must log in.

If you haven't, you usually have to register with the Web site. For most shopping Web sites, this registration is a one-time process, and the site will remember your information for future visits. You start by typing in your e-mail address, then you are asked for your shipping information (see Figure 9.9) and billing information (see Figure 9.10). You will then be asked to put in a password so that you don't have to enter all this information next time you want to order. At each step, double-check to make sure the information you have typed in is correct.

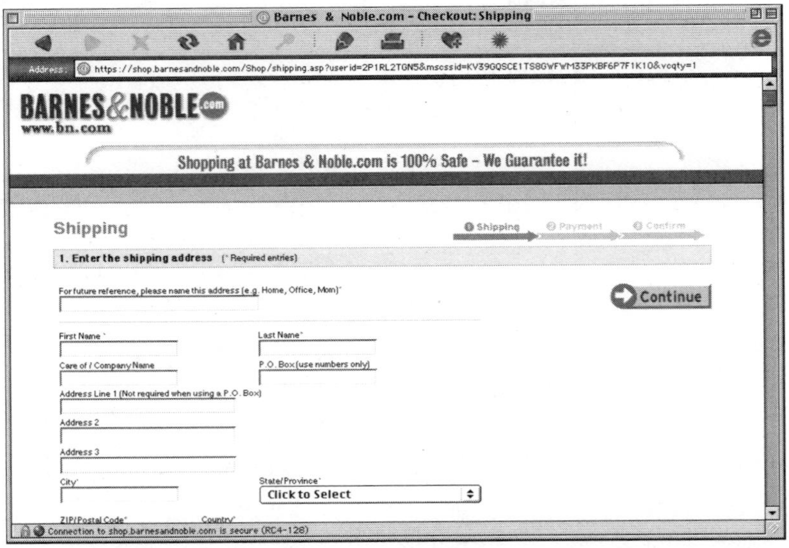

Figure 9.9
This page allows you to enter your shipping information.

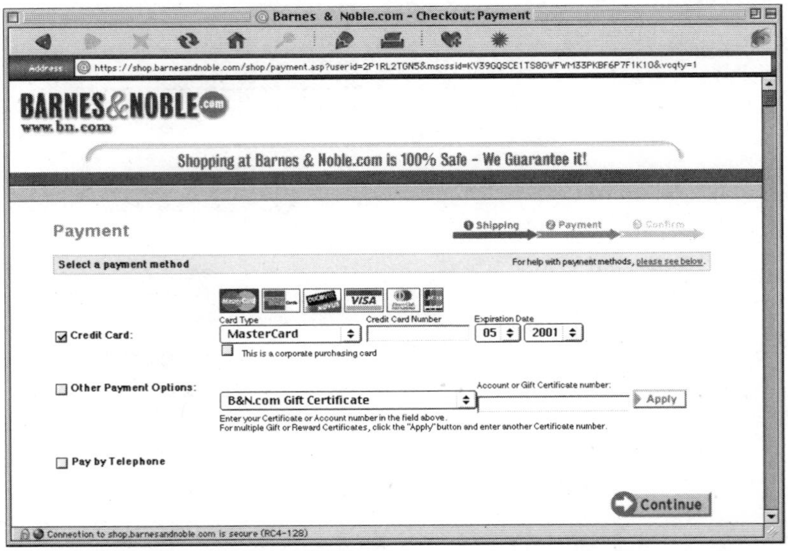

Figure 9.10
At this page, you supply your billing information.

Then, all this information is put together with your virtual shopping cart and displayed on a single page (see Figure 9.11). At this point, your order still hasn't been placed, so you still have the opportunity to change your mind.

Figure 9.11
The Barnes & Noble.com Order Confirmation page.

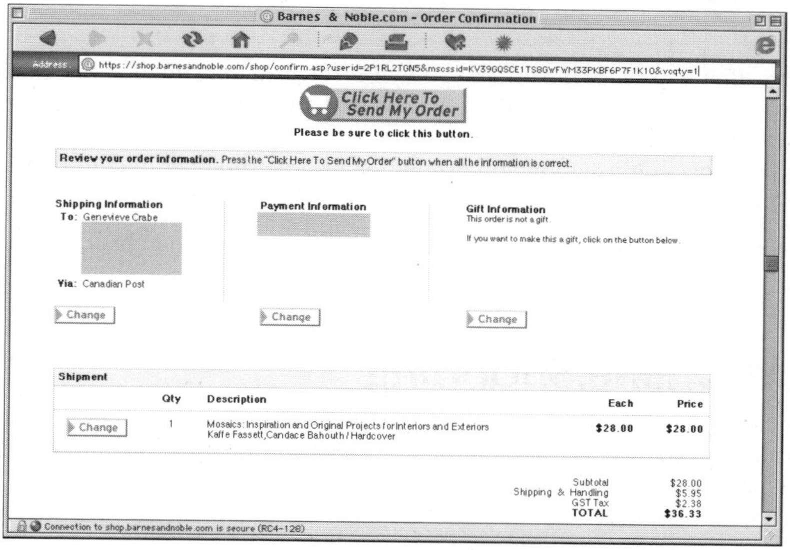

Finally, you have gotten to the point where the order will actually be placed. Click the button that says **Click Here to Send My Order** to place the order. You then get a Thank You page, where you are told that you will receive a confirmation by e-mail (see Figure 9.12). Note that most, but not all, shopping sites will send you an order confirmation by e-mail. Either way, it's good practice to print the order page, so you are sure you have a record.

Figure 9.12
The Barnes & Noble.com Confirm Order page.

TIP

When you are filling out an online form, there is usually an indication of which fields are required. Don't volunteer extra information—fill out only the necessary fields.

Shortly after you place the order, you will receive an e-mail message containing the details of your order. Keep this e-mail. If there is a problem with your order, in some cases you can simply reply to that e-mail to reach the customer service department. If not, you can use the information from the order confirmation you printed (your order number or confirmation number) to contact the company.

Some merchants will also send you an e-mail when your merchandise is shipped so that you know when to expect it.

Safe Online Shopping

If you are new to the Internet, you are probably apprehensive about giving out personal information. The fact is that in most cases your information is quite safe, especially if you follow a few precautions.

Choosing a Shopping Site

First, you can start with established vendors, i.e. companies you are familiar with, or Web sites that belong to stores that you know so that you have a "real" store you can go to if you have any problems.

Discussion groups can come in handy here, because you can ask people for shopping site recommendations. Fellow list members will happily share their online shopping experiences and recommend their favorite sites.

Understanding the Terms

Before you order, look up all the details and extra charges related to your order: the shipping and handling charges, taxes, and so on. Also remember to check the return policy.

Additionally, you want to check the site's privacy policy; there will usually be a link to it on a site's main page. This policy spells out what the company will and will not do with the personal information you provide. Also, many merchants will want you to subscribe to e-mail newsletters and allow them to give out your e-mail to other merchants The forms will usually give you the opportunity to "opt out," that is, to turn off the option to receive these newsletters. Read the form carefully to understand what you are agreeing to.

The Paper Trail

You want to make sure to keep records of all information relevant to your transaction. First of all, print out or write down real-world information about the merchant: company name, address, phone number, and any other contact information provided. When you order something, at the end of your transaction you should get a Web page with the details of your order—print this out for your records. Also, make note of the e-mail address and phone number for customer service; you can use this if you have any questions about your order. Most shopping sites will send you a confirmation e-mail.

Paying for Your Purchases

Credit cards are the method of choice for online shopping sites, and online credit card fraud is very rare. But if you don't have a credit card, or don't want to use one online, many sites will allow you to pay by check or money order. They will take your order online and wait until they receive your payment before they ship the merchandise.

Although many sites allow you to use a check or money order, you should understand that using a credit card actually gives you the best protection, because credit card companies will protect you against fraud or misuse of your card, and your liability is limited. Check the specific terms of your credit card account for details. If you feel uneasy about using your credit card online, many merchants will allow you to put in your order online and then phone them with your credit card number.

To make it easier to track online purchases, you might consider getting a separate credit card that you use only on the Internet. Furthermore, with many credit cards, you can check your transactions and statements online. With this feature, you can check the activity on your credit card at any time, rather than waiting for your monthly statement.

Secure Ordering

Online credit card shopping on a secure Web site is as safe as or safer than credit card shopping in a store or restaurant. There are two main fears about using credit cards online: having someone intercept your credit card number and then misuse it and getting charged for merchandise you never received. The first risk is minimized by using a secure Web page, and the second is usually taken care of by the credit card company. In case your credit card number is misused, your liability is quite limited, sometimes zero. Each credit card company has its own policy on this, so you'll need to check the specific terms of your credit card. You should be able to find these policies online; look for the name of your bank or credit card using your search engine.

So, what is a secure Web page? It's a Web page that use a technology called Secure Socket Layer (SSL) to encrypt the information you send using a complex mathematical process; when the information reaches its destination, it is decoded. If this sounds complicated, simply remember that this makes it impossible for someone to intercept your information, like a credit card number, in a useful form.

Now, how do you tell if a Web page is secure? Somewhere in your browser window, usually in the lower left corner, you will see a picture of an open padlock (or a broken key, or no padlock). If the page you are looking at is a secure page, the padlock is closed (or the key is not broken). Figure 9.13 shows a non-secure page and a secure page with the padlock image.

Figure 9.13
Padlock in browser
window.

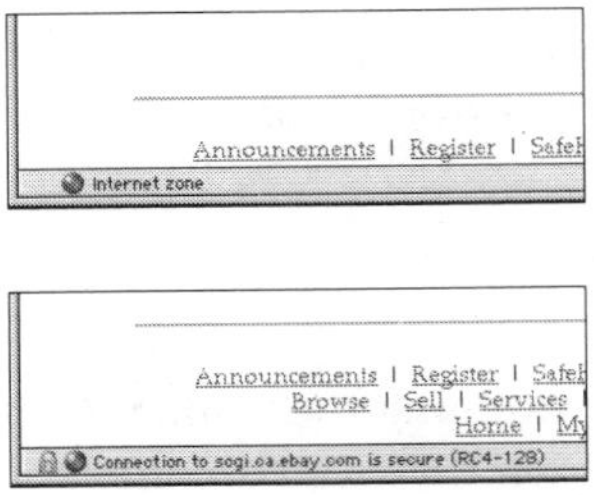

If you look back at our Barnes & Noble order, you can see the secure pages in Figures 9.8 through 9.12.

TIP

It's not necessary for all the pages on a Web site to be secure, only the one where you enter your personal information.

The second way to tell if a page is secure is by the page's address or URL. Look in the address or location bar of your browser. If you are on a non-secure page, the URL begins with "http," but if you are on a secure page, the URL begins with "https".

In order to make sure you are using the most up-to-date encryption in your browser, you should run the latest version of the browser. Here are the sites where you can obtain the latest browsers:

Internet Explorer for Windows: **http://www.microsoft.com/windows/ie/**
Internet Explorer for Macintosh: **http://www.microsoft.com/mac/ie/**
Netscape: **http://home.netscape.com/browsers/**

CAUTION

Never send your credit card number by e-mail. This is not a secure way to send information.

Cookies

Some shopping sites will tell you that they use "cookies" to keep track of your information. So what are these cookies, anyway?

A cookie is a small piece of information that a Web site stores on your computer in order to remember you and what you have been doing on the site. For example, you may have noticed that some Web sites where you have shopped know your name when you return. This is because they left a cookie on your machine when you first visited; when you return, the site checks for this cookie and is then able to display your name. Figure 9.14 shows an example; I often shop at ArtistsClub.com, and you can see that it uses my name in the Welcome message.

Figure 9.14
ArtistsClub.com
"remembers" me.

Cookies can be used to remember more extensive information. For example, you might go to a shopping site, put a few items in your virtual shopping cart, and then leave before placing the order. On some sites, if you return at a later time, the contents of your shopping cart are still there; that's because the site left a cookie containing all that information on your computer.

Your Account

Some of the larger commerce Web sites let you set up an account, and this can greatly simplify your shopping experience. The first time you visit, you enter your shipping and billing information, and then you are asked to enter a password. On future visits, you simply enter your e-mail address and password, and the rest of the information is retrieved and filled into the form for you.

TIP
There are two simple rules to follow when choosing a password: It should be easy for you to remember and difficult for others to guess.

After you have placed an order, many sites will let you come back to the site and check on the status of your order, and even track the shipment.

For More Information...

The Internet offers many resources to help you find out information about businesses. The Better Business Bureau at **http://www.bbb.org/** (see Figure 9.15) lets you check out a company or file a complaint against one. The BBB also has a page with online shopping tips at **http://www.bbb.org/library/shoponline.asp**.

Figure 9.15
Better Business Bureau has resources to help you decide whether an online business is trustworthy.

You can also visit one of the following sites for business information as well as information on how to avoid fraud and scams:

Federal Trade Commission
http://www.ftc.gov/

Canadian Office of Consumer Affairs
http://strategis.ic.gc.ca/sc_consu/consaffairs/engdoc/oca.html

National Fraud Information Center
http://www.fraud.org/

Internet Scambusters
http://www.scambusters.org/

RCMP Information on Scams
http://www.rcmp-grc.gc.ca/scams/scams.htm

Cross-Border Shopping

In the U.S. and Canada, we often buy from vendors that are across the border from us, and this introduces extra expenses you need to be aware of, including increased shipping charges, duty, and taxes. You need to take all this into account in figuring out if you are getting a good deal.

Sometimes, cost is not the only consideration; it could be convenience or speed of delivery, or perhaps the only vendor who sells the items you are looking for is across the border. Whatever your reason for cross-border shopping, watch out for duty and extra taxes, and make sure you understand the shipping charges, which will likely be more than they are when you order domestically.

TIP

Before you buy, check whether the site offers shipping across the border. Some don't, and this information is not always displayed prominently.

For information on duty and taxes, again you can use the Internet. In the U.S., go to the United States Customs Service at **http://www.customs.ustreas.gov/** (see Figure 9.16).

Figure 9.16
The U.S. Customs
Service home page.

In Canada, you can visit the Canada Customs and Revenue Agency web site at **http://www.ccra-adrc.gc.ca/** (see Figure 9.17).

Figure 9.17
The Canada Customs
and Revenue Agency
home page.

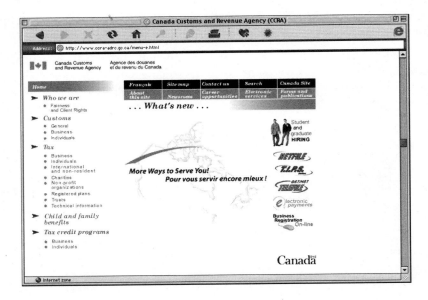

In addition to duty and taxes, you must consider brokerage fees, which will vary according to the shipping carrier used by the merchant. These are charged by the carrier for taking your package across the border and figuring out the duty, taxes, and so on.

There is some good news, though. Some online merchants will pay the duty for you, and some will handle the transfer of the merchandise across the border so that you don't have to pay brokerage fees. Artistsclub.com is an example of a U.S. company that makes it easy to order from Canada.

10
Finding Supplies

In the previous chapter, we learned about the ins and outs of online shopping. In this chapter, we will see how to apply these new skills to shopping for craft supplies.

Why would you want to buy crafting supplies online? The Internet offers countless choices, both in merchants and in merchandise. You can shop around for the best deals and have several sources for the supplies you need.

Even if you have local sources for your supplies, having online sources can be a useful alternative. On the one hand, you may want to keep track of which of your suppliers have the best prices for general shopping; on the other hand, you can also keep track of those who can ship the fastest, for those times when you need things in a hurry for a class or a craft show.

Searching for Online Suppliers

You can use a search engine to find supplies, by using appropriate search words to narrow your search as we learned in Chapter 3. For example, say you want to find woodworking supplies online. Figure 10.1 shows that when you search simply for the word "woodworking" using the Google Search engine, you get 415,000 results.

Figure 10.1
Search: woodworking.

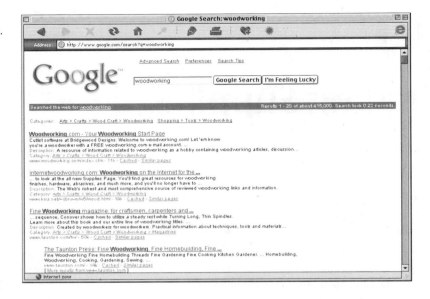

Now, let's search for "woodworking supplies." As you can see in Figure 10.2, the search has been narrowed down to 69,300 results.

Figure 10.2
Search: woodworking supplies.

You can use other words, such as "shopping," to narrow the search further. Using more words can narrow the search even more. In Figure 10.3, searching for "woodworking" along with the phrase "online shopping" returns around 3,000 results.

Figure 10.3
Google Search:
woodworking
"online shopping."

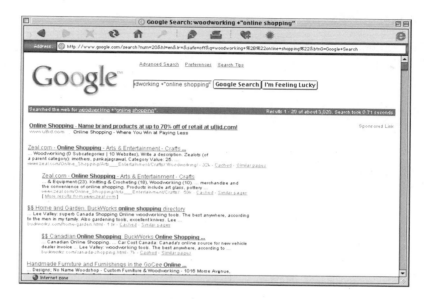

On About.com, the Craft Supply Search Network at **http://artsandcrafts.about.com/ blcraftsupply.htm** (see Figure 10.4) can help you locate supplies if you have been having trouble locating them on your own.

Figure 10.4
About.com's Craft
Supply Search
Network helps you
search more effectively.

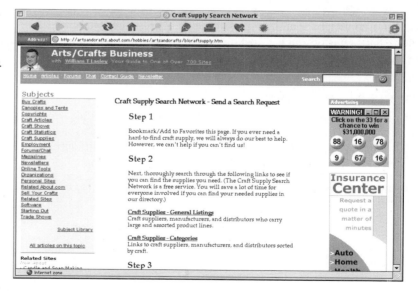

It consists of lists of suppliers for you to try, and if you still can't find what you are looking for, you can fill out a form (see Figure 10.5). This is a free service that will search for a supplier of the items you are looking for.

Figure 10.5
The Craft Supply
Search Network
search form.

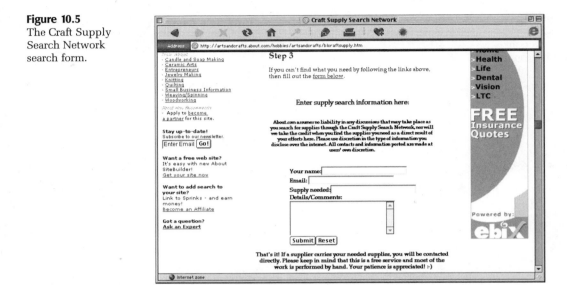

There is also a discussion group (forum) where you can post your request.

Locating Products

In addition to using a search engine, there are many other ways the Internet can be useful for locating particular products. Most of the manufacturers of craft supplies have their own Web sites, as do most retail outlets.

Product Manufacturers

Most product manufacturers have their own Web sites, and the URLs are fairly easy to find. You can usually find the URL on packaging or instruction booklets, or use your search engine to look for the company name. Sometimes, you will see an advertisement in a magazine for a particular product, along with the URL for the manufacturer's Web site.

For example, I recently saw an ad for Tulip fabric paint that gave the URL for Duncan Enterprises (see Figure 10.6).

Figure 10.6
This manufacturer, Duncan Enterprises, can guide you to places where its products are sold.

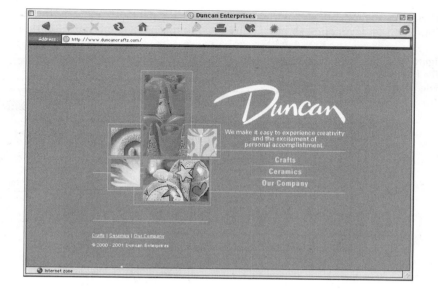

By using the Product Locator on the site, I was able to find the list of stores that carry the paint (see Figure 10.7).

Figure 10.7
Duncan Enterprises' Product Locator.

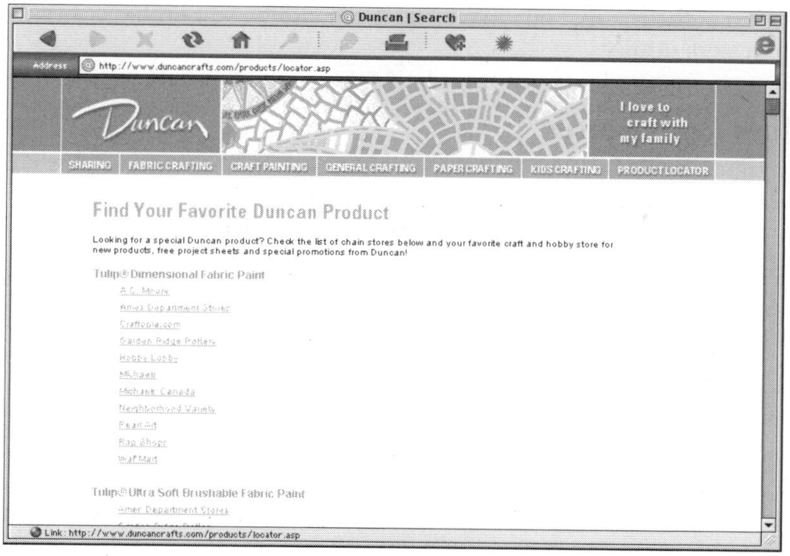

This gives me a list of stores that carry the paint. Each store name on the list is itself a Web link. For example, I can click Hobby Lobby to go to that Web site (Figure 10.8)

Figure 10.8
The Hobby Lobby
home page.

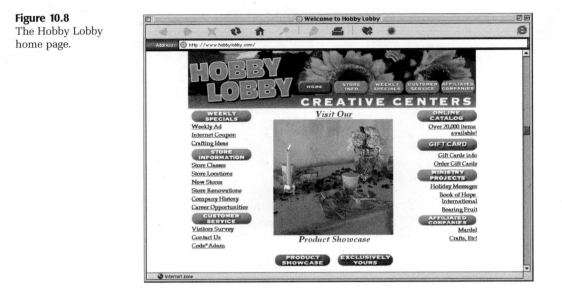

Once I am at the Hobby Lobby Web site, I can either shop online or use the Store Locations link to find a store nearby.

Online Craft Stores

The companion Web site provides a lot of links to online craft suppliers. Some of them, like Michael's and Hobby Lobby, are associated with conventional stores that you may be familiar with, and others are "virtual" stores, which means that they exist only on the Internet.

Some stores, like Crafts Etc. at **http://www.craftsetc.com/** (see Figure 10.9), are general stores that sell supplies for a variety of crafts.

Figure 10.9
Crafts Etc. sells a wide
variety of supplies.

Others are specialized, like ArtistsClub at **http://www.artistsclub.com/** (see Figure 10.10), which
sells decorative painting supplies, and Herrschners at **http://www.herrschners.com/** (see Figure
10.11), which sells needlecraft supplies.

Figure 10.10
ArtistsClub is a
specialized supply site.

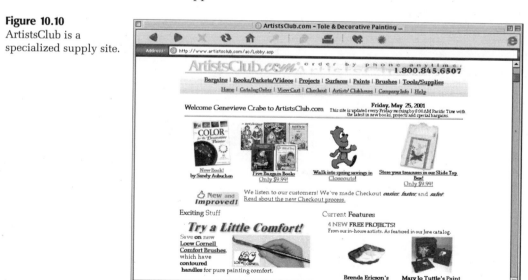

Figure 10.11
Herrschners sells
needlecraft supplies.

Plaid Enterprises manufactures a wide range of craft supplies. Their Web site, at
http://www.plaidonline.com/, includes projects complete with supply lists. Figure 10.12 is an
example of a project; you can see on the right the list of Plaid supplies you need for this project
(paint, brushes, varnish, and so on).

Figure 10.12
Plaid offers projects as
well as supplies.

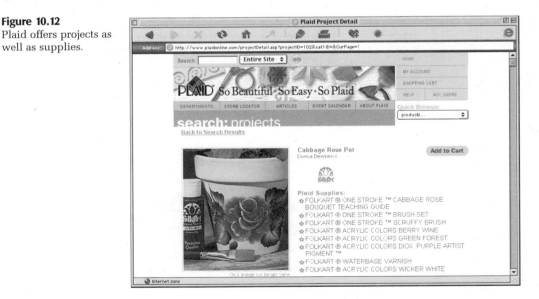

Bookstores

Crafters usually buy lots of books. This is where we find inspiration, project ideas, techniques, and more. The Internet provides many new sources of books for you to explore. There are bookstores, publishers, even used bookstores online.

Amazon.com at **http://amazon.com/** (see Figure 10.13) is one of the better known online bookstores. Many chains also have their online stores, like Barnes & Noble, which we visited in Chapter 9. You will find more URLs on the companion Web site.

Figure 10.13
Amazon.com.

While many Canadians often shop at stores across the border, we do have our own online bookstores, like Chapters at **http://www.chapters.ca/**.

Used bookstores are another great source for books. You can find current books at discount prices, and used bookstores are a source for copies of out-of-print books. The Advanced Book Exchange (abebooks) at **http://www.abebooks.com/** (Figure 10.14) illustrates how the power of the Internet can be used in business.

Figure 10.14
The abebooks.com
Web site brings
together thousands
of used bookstores.

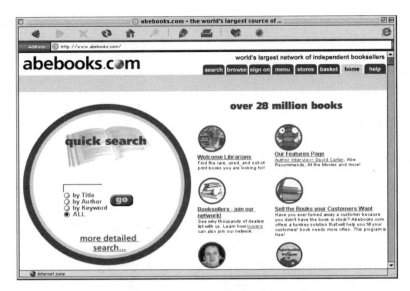

Abebooks has created a Web site that is a network of thousands of used bookstores in several countries. It helps to connect buyers with sellers by creating a database containing the combined inventory of all the member booksellers.

For example, I did a search for books by decorative artist Priscilla Hauser. As you can see in Figure 10.15, there are several copies of the same books available from different sources, so comparison shopping is very easy. The book description includes the condition of the book, so you can decide based on the condition of books or on the prices.

Figure 10.15
Abebooks
Search Results.

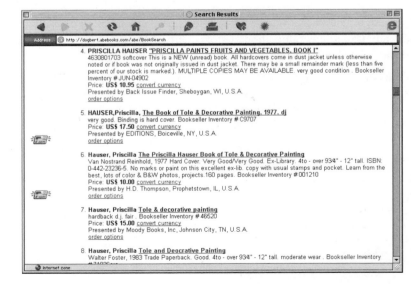

Additionally, you can purchase books from craft supply stores online or directly from some craft book publishers.

Television

There are a lot of craft shows on television, in addition to crafting segments on home decorating and other shows. Most of these shows have Web sites that include information about the guests, products, and the projects shown. Let's look at the Carol Duvall Show as an example.

To find the Carol Duvall show online, go to **http://www.hgtv.com/**, click HGTV Show List, and then click Carol Duvall (see Figure 10.16).

Figure 10.16
HGTV's Carol Duvall Show has a Web site.

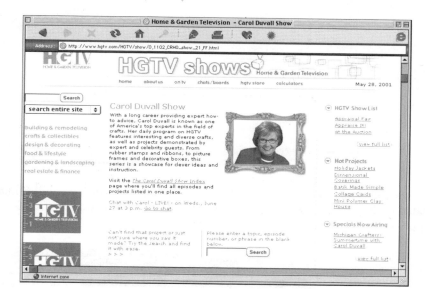

The Web site contains pages for all the projects shown on the show. Let's search for a project I saw recently called Needlepoint Mosaic. Enter this in the Search box and hit Enter to find the project page (see Figure 10.17).

Figure 10.17
Carol Duvall—
Needlepoint Mosaic
Project, part 1.

If you scroll down to the bottom of the page (see Figure 10.18), you will find a list of resources related to the project. These include a link to the designer's Web site, as well as links to suppliers of materials required for the project.

Figure 10.18
Carol Duvall—
Needlepoint Mosaic
Project, part 2.

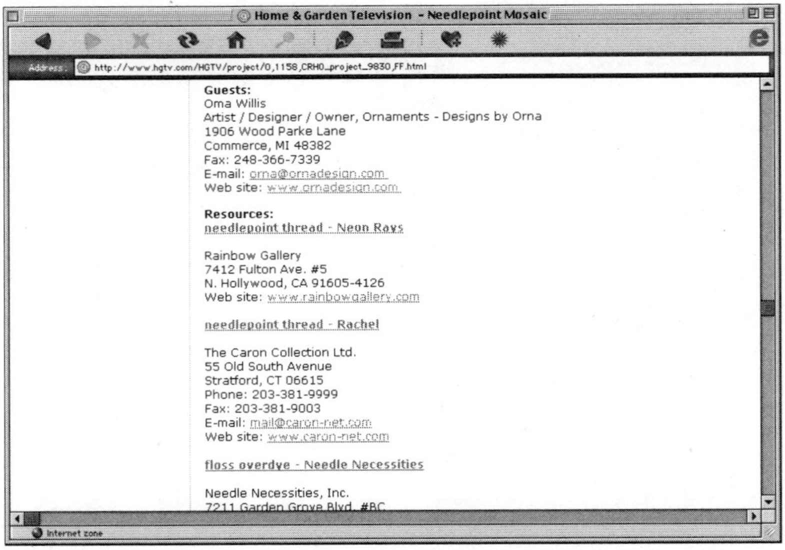

The television shopping channels—such as QVC at **http://www.iqvc.com/** in the U.S. (see Figure 10.19) and The Shopping Channel at **http://www.theshoppingchannel.com/** in Canada (see Figure 10.20)—often feature craft products and include great demonstrations in the shows that feature those products.

Figure 10.19
QVC online is known as iQVC.

Both QVC and The Shopping Channel have craft programming where they offer special kits that are usually not available elsewhere.

Figure 10.20
The Shopping Channel's Web site.

If you have ever spent any time on hold waiting to place a telephone order, you will appreciate the fact that both shopping channels offer online ordering on their Web sites. An extra service if you order online is an e-mail notification when your order is shipped, so you will have a better idea when you will receive it. Depending on your shipping option, you may also be provided with a tracking number and instructions telling you how to track the shipment online.

TIP

The Internet can also help you to keep up with what is happening on your favorite shopping channel; you can subscribe to e-mail newsletters that will notify you of upcoming events.

Auctions

You may have heard about auction Web sites used by collectors to buy and sell collectible items. You may not be aware, though, that auction sites have now grown to the point where all sorts of things are bought and sold every day. In the next chapter, we'll see how you can use auction sites to sell your finished crafts, but for now let's see what we can find that we might want to buy.

I used an auction site called eBay for the first time a few months ago, and I was surprised to find how many items were available that would be of interest to crafters, from out-of-print books to brand-new craft supplies like stencils and cross-stitch patterns. Some are sold by people who are simply selling stuff they bought and didn't use; others are people who buy at wholesale or at closeout sales and resell the merchandise at auction.

Let's have a look at how eBay works.

NOTE

Since I am registered with eBay-Canada at **http://www.ebay.ca/**, this is what I will be using for the examples in this section. If you use the main eBay site at **http://www.ebay.com/**, the pages you see will be very similar.

Getting Started

Figure 10.21 shows the main page at **http://www.ebay.ca/**. The featured items on this page change frequently, so the page will not look exactly the same when you visit.

Figure 10.21
eBay—the main page.

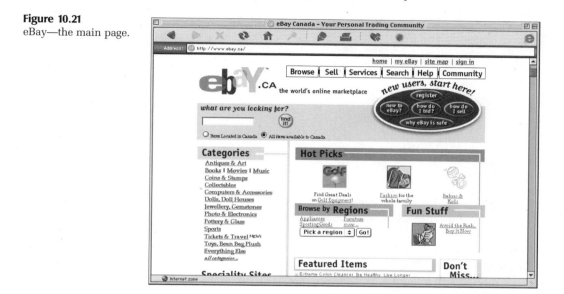

If you want to use eBay, first you will have to register. Look at the area titled "new users, start here!" at the upper right of the home page. This area contains a great amount of information to get you started. Click "register," and you will be taken through a step-by-step process to register on eBay.

Browsing

As a buyer, the first thing you want to do is see what is available. From the main page, you can simply browse through the categories. At the top of the page, click Browse. If you scroll down a bit, you will see a long list of categories. You can see the beginning of the list in Figure 10.22; the page scrolls down four more screens.

Figure 10.22
eBay—categories.

If you scroll down to the main category called "Everything Else" and then click "Crafts, Sewing," you will see the sub-categories, which include both finished crafts and craft supplies (see Figure 10.23). The numbers in parentheses indicate the number of items available in that category.

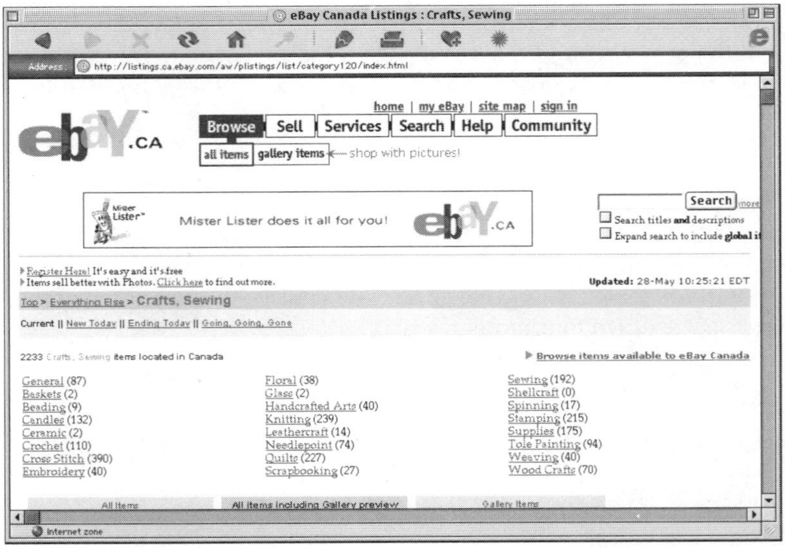

Figure 10.23
eBay—craft
sub-categories.

You can click on a category to see a list of items. Browsing is a good way to look around to find out what sorts of things are available, but if you are looking for something specific, then you want to use the search function.

Searching

Click the "Search" button at the top of the page to go to the search page (see Figure 10.24).

Figure 10.24
eBay—the search page.

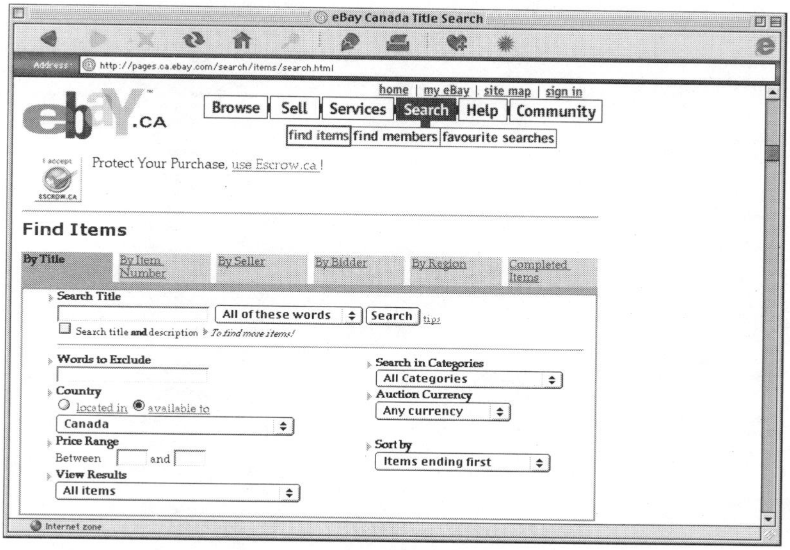

The main item you want to use for your search is the Title. Sellers on eBay go to great lengths to compose a title that is likely to contain the words people will be searching for.

Here is a quick description of some of the other elements of the search form:

► The checkbox under the title field allows you to search not only the titles of items but their descriptions as well. This will return more results.

► Under "Words to Exclude," you can specify words to omit from your search. For example, say you want to search for cross-stitch patterns but are not interested in cartoon characters. You could put in "cross-stitch" in the title field and "cartoon" in the Words to Exclude field.

► The "Country" button shows up on eBay Canada, but you won't see it on the U.S. site. On the Canadian site, it allows you to decide whether you want to search for only sellers that are *in* Canada, or search for any seller who will ship *to* Canada.

► "Search in Categories" lets you search only in a specific category. For example, since we know the craft stuff is in the "Everything Else" category, you can select that to narrow the search. On the other hand, some people will sometimes put their items in the wrong category, so you might not want to limit yourself.

► There are other ways to search—for example, "By seller." This is something you might do after you have used eBay a few times and are familiar with particular sellers.

Now, let's do a search and see if we can find something we might want to bid on. I want to get a stencil of a column for a home decorating project, so I enter "stencil column" in the title field and click "Search." Figure 10.25 shows the search results.

Figure 10.25
eBay—Search results
for "stencil column."

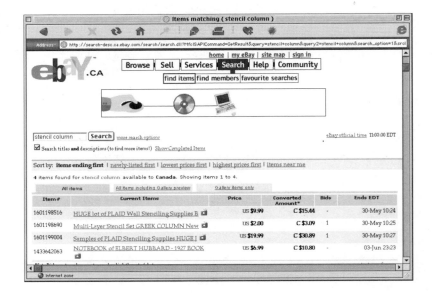

The multi-layer Greek column stencil item looks promising, so I click the title and get the item details, as shown in Figure 10.26.

Figure 10.26
eBay—an Item page.

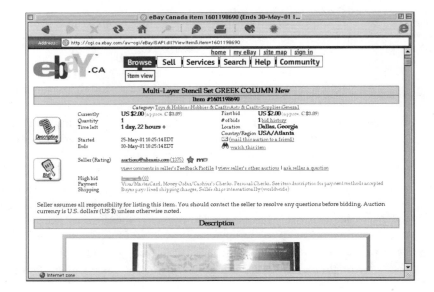

The top part of the page shows details about the item, including the current bid and the amount of time left in the auction. There is also some information about the seller, where he resides, and his identification (in this case, the seller's e-mail address). Scroll down a bit, and you will see the description of the item, which usually includes a picture.

The number in parentheses next to the seller's identification represents the number of positive feedback messages that this person has received. After every transaction, both buyer and seller are invited to submit feedback comments about the transaction. A person's feedback rating can help you decide whether you want to do business with this person. In this case, this seller has received well over 1,000 positive feedback comments, and you can read those comments by clicking the number.

After checking the feedback, I decide that I want to bid on this item.

Bidding

Scroll down to the bottom of the page to the Bidding section (see Figure 10.27); this is where I will be placing my bid.

Figure 10.27
eBay—Item bidding.

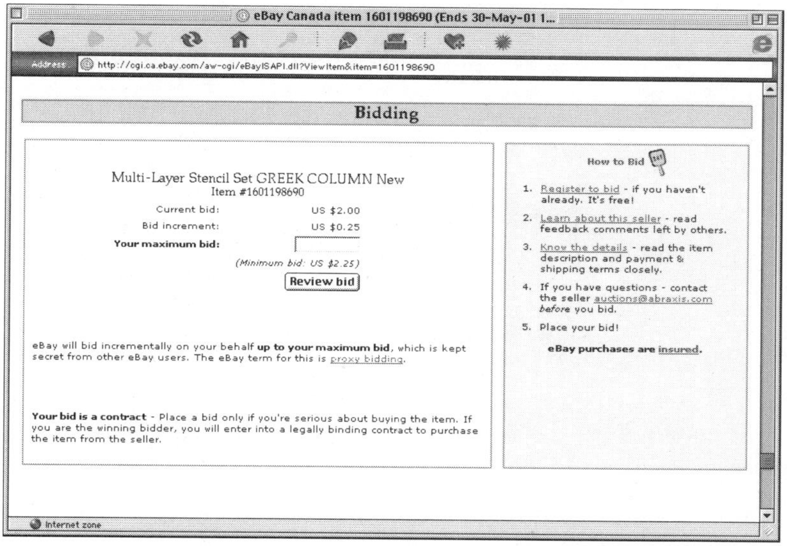

Before going any further, though, I have to explain "proxy bidding," which allows you to specify your maximum bid and have the eBay system automatically bid for you until your maximum is reached.

Here is how it works in our example:

You saw in Figure 10.26 that the current bid is $2.00 and the minimum bid I can put in is $2.25. Say I put in $2.25, then someone outbids me, then I bid again, and on and on until the end of the auction.

Section IV Buying Online

eBay has a way to make this process easier. Instead of bidding the minimum $2.25, I decide that the maximum I want to pay for this item is $5.00, and this is the amount I entered in the page on Figure 10.27. This amount is not made public. When I click "Review Bid," I get a confirmation page and I approve the bid.

Automatically, eBay bids the minimum $2.25 on my behalf. Then it looks for other bidders' maximum bids and automatically bids for them. Eventually, either I will remain the high bidder or my $5.00 will be exceeded by someone else's maximum bid.

In this example, my bid went up to $3.25 (Figure 10.28), and I am still the high bidder.

Check the Help section on eBay for a more detailed explanation of proxy bidding.

Figure 10.28
eBay—Item bidding
confirmation.

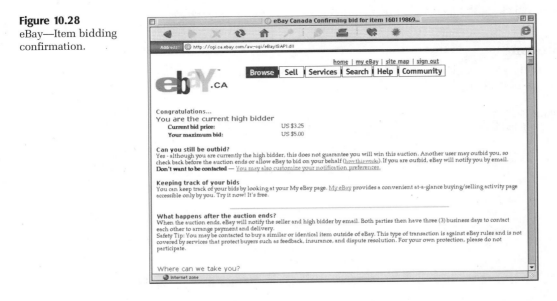

You will receive an e-mail confirming your bid. You will also receive an e-mail to let you know if you are outbid. If you are the high bidder when the auction ends, you will receive an e-mail notifying you that you have won the auction.

You Won! What Now?

When you receive a notification that you have won an auction, the next step is to contact the seller. After that, you work out the details of payment and shipping.

When you receive the merchandise, remember to leave feedback about the seller. Most sellers will do the same for you.

TIP

Auction Buying Tips

▶ Always check the seller's rating before bidding.

▶ Don't get carried away and pay more than the item would cost at retail.

▶ Watch out for people who will try to outbid you at the last minute.

▶ Make sure that the shipping and payment options are suitable before you bid.

▶ If you have any questions, contact the seller by e-mail before you bid.

▶ Some people on eBay are involved in many transactions at once. To make things easier, make sure you include the item number (it's under the title in Figure 10.25) in all correspondence.

My eBay

If you have several auctions in progress, you want an easy way to keep track of them. Click "my eBay" at the top of the page and you get a page (see Figure 10.29) that shows you all the auctions you are currently participating in.

Figure 10.29

eBay—My eBay page.

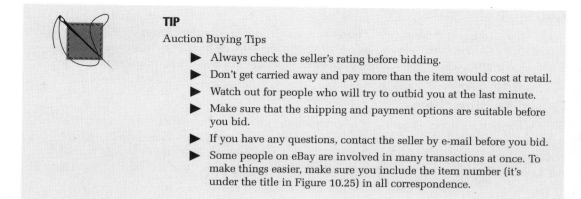

There is another feature of My eBay you may find useful. Look back to Figure 10.26 and you will see a link called "watch this item" that you can use to keep track of this item. You are not bidding on it, but the item will appear on your My eBay page so you can keep an eye on it. We'll talk about this feature again in the next section.

Getting Help

If you click "Help" at the top of any page, you will find helpful information on all areas of eBay. If you click "Community," also at the top of the page, you will find more resources, such as discussion groups where you can exchange information with and get help from other users.

Other Auction Sites

Ebay is by far the largest and most popular auction site. There are other auction sites, like Amazon.com auctions at **http://auctions.amazon.com/,** which has associated itself with Sotheby's, the famous auction house. The second largest auction site, after eBay, is Yahoo! Auctions, at **http://auctions.yahoo.com/,** which includes Yahoo!'s great search capabilities.

Business Shopping

If you are a business crafter, the Internet is a good place to find wholesale suppliers. You can use a search engine and include the items you are looking for and add the word "wholesale" to your search. Shopping isn't any different from what we have seen already, except that with wholesale suppliers, you usually must purchase minimum quantities.

Additionally, you can use shipping companies' Web sites to manage your shipping. The companion Web site contains some links to some of the major shipping companies, and you can find more by using a search engine. One of the advantages of using a shipping company's Web site is that you can track your packages online.

Other supplies you can find online for your business include computer hardware, software, stationery, and packaging materials.

Section V
Selling and Marketing Online

"Shoot for the moon. Even if you miss, you'll land among the stars."

—Les Brown

11
What to Sell Online

In this chapter, we're going to talk about how the Internet can help you do market research for your business. If you want to collect information about your customer base, your competitors, market trends, and so on, the Internet is a great place to start. We're not just talking about setting up an Internet-based business here. Even if your business is a conventional one, the Internet has a lot to offer.

Market research is what helps you answer questions about what, where, and to whom to sell.

Craft Business Information

If you know where (or how) to look, there is a tremendous amount of information available online regarding the business side of crafting.

As with other topics, one place you can start is About.com. There is an area entirely dedicated to this topic at **http://artsandcrafts.about.com/** (see Figure 11.1).

Figure 11.1
Arts & Crafts Business on About.com helps you be a better business person.

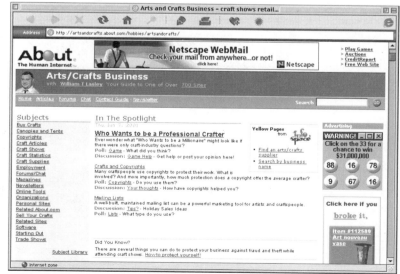

This topic area on About.com contains a lot of articles and links to useful Web sites, as well as discussion forums on all aspects of the crafting business. Start by scanning the list of topics on the left. For example, if you're new to the crafting business world, the Starting Out section (see Figure 11.2) contains several articles on starting either a conventional business or an Internet-based one.

Figure 11.2
Arts & Crafts
Business—Starting Out.

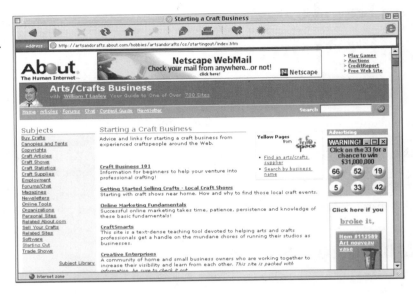

Another great resource is The Crafts Report magazine Web site at **http://www.craftsreport.com/** (see Figure 11.3).

Figure 11.3
The Crafts Report
Web site supplements
the national business
magazine.

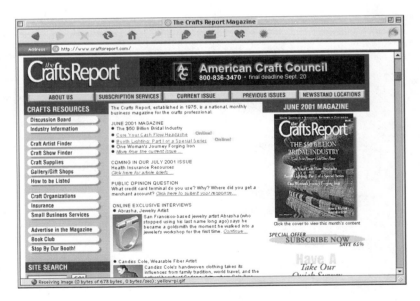

There are pages on this site where you can find craft shows in your area, suppliers, craft organizations, and more. Although this is information that is probably available elsewhere, the Internet makes it all much more easily accessible.

There are even sites on the Web that are dedicated to information about the craft business. One such site is CraftSmarts at **http://www.craftsmarts.com/** (see Figure 11.4), where John Iverson shares his expertise on the craft business, based on twenty years' experience in the crafts industry.

Figure 11.4
CraftSmarts draws on personal experience in the crafts industry.

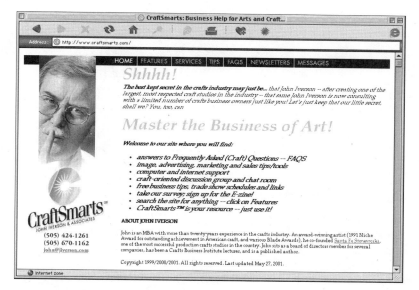

Section V Selling and Marketing Online

Before the Internet, interactions like this would have been impossible. Now, you can network with people all over the world. You can find more sites like this by looking for "craft business" in your favorite search engine.

Another great source of information is in the contacts you make in discussion groups (discussed in Chapter 6). People are usually quite willing to share their expertise and their experience.

In addition to crafting business information sites, you can find a lot of useful information on sites that offer general information on small business. For example, Entrepreneur.com (see Figure 11.5), which is affiliated with Entrepreneur magazine, contains a wealth of information, as well as business tools, such as downloadable financial and legal forms.

Figure 11.5
Entrepreneur.com
offers general
information on running
a small business.

There are also small-business sites on About.com at **http://sbinformation.about.com** for the U.S. and **http://sbinfocanada.about.com/** for Canada.

Finally, you can find official government information on the U.S. Government Business Advisor site at **http://www.business.gov/** (see Figure 11.6) and the Industry Canada Business and Consumer site at **http://strategis.ic.gc.ca/** (see Figure 11.7).

Figure 11.6
U.S. Business Advisor
contains official
government
information…

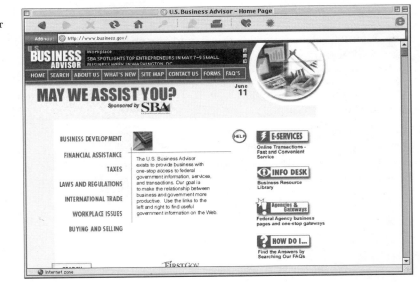

Figure 11.7
… as does Industry
Canada.

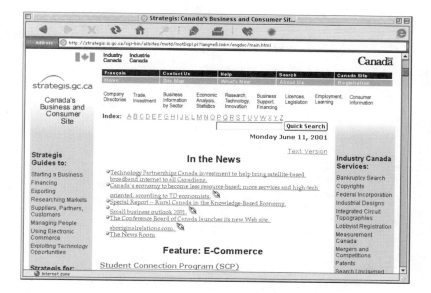

Section V Selling and Marketing Online

Deciding What to Sell

Currently, you might figure out what to sell by visiting local shops and seeing what they offer, going to craft shows, and talking to other crafters in your area. The Internet allows you to expand this search in a big way.

In the next chapter, we'll talk about how to sell on the Internet, but whether you are interested in selling online or not, you can use the Internet to research what is currently selling well. You can do that by visiting sites on the Web where crafts are sold, such as specialty craft sites and online giftware shops. In your search engine, you can use general words like "giftware," "shopping," or "handmade" along with words that represent your craft.

Here is an instance where a precise choice of search words can make a big difference. In Figure 11.8, I did a search on the words "shopping" and "quilting." The results I got were mainly Web sites that sell quilting supplies.

Figure 11.8
Results from a search
for "shopping quilting."

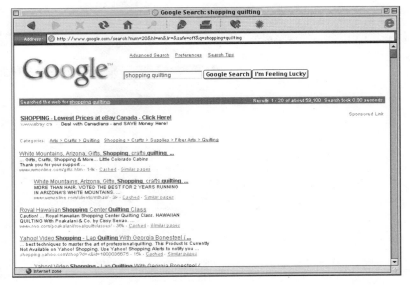

In Figure 11.9, I did a search on the words "shopping" and "quilts." This time, I got sites that sell finished quilts. This shows that your choice of words in a search can make a big difference, and if you don't get the results you expected right away, you can try variations of your search words.

Figure 11.9
Results of a search for
"shopping quilts."

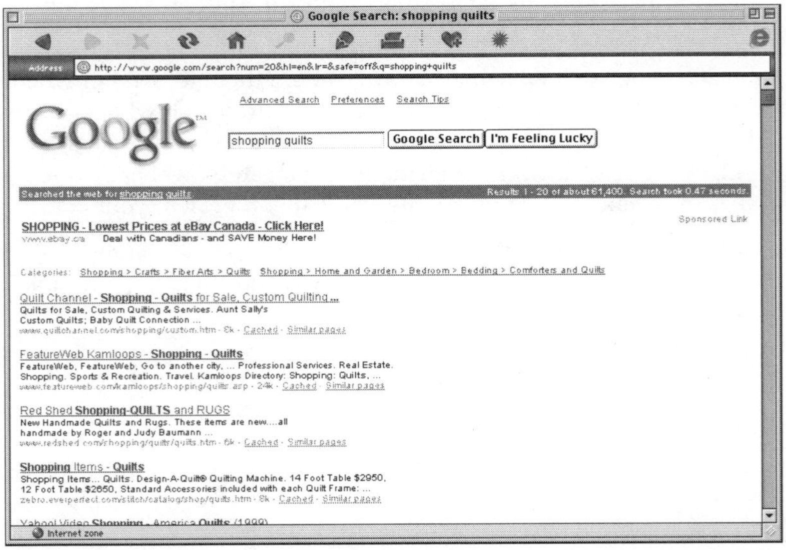

You can also ask participants in discussion lists about their craft show experiences. This will give you a broader view than the one you get in your local area.

Auction sites are another source of good information. You can look for items that are similar to the ones that you want to sell and watch them to see how well they do.

As far as selling on the Internet is concerned, there are several ways to do that, as we'll see in Chapter 12. Just about any item you sell in a store or craft show can be sold on the Internet, although it might be difficult to sell bulky or heavy items because of shipping considerations.

You can sell finished crafts, craft supplies, or pattern packets. If you are selling a tangible product, selling on the Internet has a lot in common with catalogue sales—except the catalogue is online instead of on paper.

Selling Patterns

Pattern Packets are craft project instructions that are packaged for sale. They usually include a photo of the finished project, a list of supplies needed, a chart if required, and an instructions sheet. Now, you can sell pattern packets online the same way you do in a store, having people order them and then shipping them out, but there is an alternative you might want to consider.

You could sell downloadable patterns. What does this mean? It means that the pattern is stored in electronic form, and when customers purchase the pattern online, they then simply download the pattern, which means they get a copy of these electronic documents on their computer. They can then print the pattern themselves on their own printer. This works for decorative painting patterns, needlework charts, and many other craft projects.

The documents containing your pattern should be in a format that can be used by anyone. The format most commonly used for such things is Portable Document Format (PDF). In Chapter 4, I described some software you can use to convert your existing documents to PDF format. You can also look into Adobe Acrobat at **http://www.adobe.com/**.

Selling patterns electronically has several advantages for you: You don't need to print copies of the patterns yourself, and you have nothing to ship. For your customers, the advantage is that they can buy a pattern and get it immediately, rather than having to wait for it to be shipped.

Trends

The Internet is also a great place to find information about market trends. Although you can look at what is selling right now by visiting online shopping sites, you can also tap into some market research that will help you figure out what will sell in the future.

On About.com, there is a section devoted to statistical information about the crafting industry. This page can be found at **http://artsandcrafts.about.com/hobbies/artsandcrafts/cs/craftstatistics/** (see Figure 11.10).

Section V Selling and Marketing Online

Figure 11.10
About.com provides trend information at its Craft Industry Statistics page.

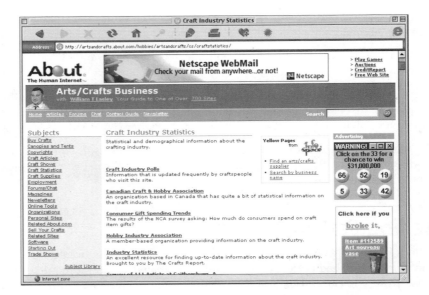

There are U.S. and Canadian reports, polls, and survey results, all of which can supply useful information. You can also go to craft associations like the Hobby Industry Association at **http://www.hobby.org/** or the National Craft Association Business Resource Center at **http://www.craftassoc.com/** for industry news, information about the crafting business, and research reports. You'll find many more association Web links on the companion Web site.

There are also industry magazines aimed at the business crafter and—you guessed it—these magazines have a presence on the Web. Craftrends, online at **http://www.craftrends.com/** (see Figure 11.11), offers information on the craft marketplace, wholesale suppliers, and more.

Figure 11.11
Craftrends magazine has a companion Web site.

Sunshine Artist, at **http://sunshineartist.com/** (see Figure 11.12), offers business and marketing tips, interactive forums, and other useful information.

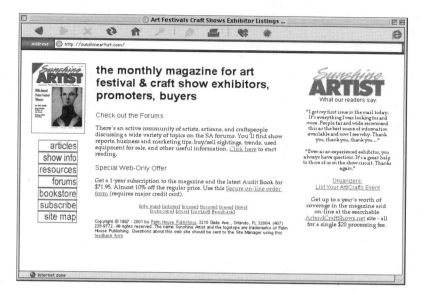

For even more information on market trends, you can look for information on specific areas related to the kinds of crafts you make. For example, if you create home decorating pieces, you can use your search engine to look for market trends in the home decorating market. If you create wearable items, then you want to look for market trends in the fashion industry. The giftware industry is another area where you can find useful information on your potential market.

Here is an example of a site containing information that could be of interest to all crafters. The major focus of Color Marketing Group (CMG) is to identify the direction of color trends in design for the next three years or so. You can find this information on its Web site at **http://www.colormarketing.org/** (see Figure 11.13).

Figure 11.13
The Color Marketing Group forecasts color trends in design.

Another site with information you might find useful is American Demographics, at **http://www.demographics.com/** (see Figure 11.14) where you can find statistical information on trends that can help you determine what kind of products to sell.

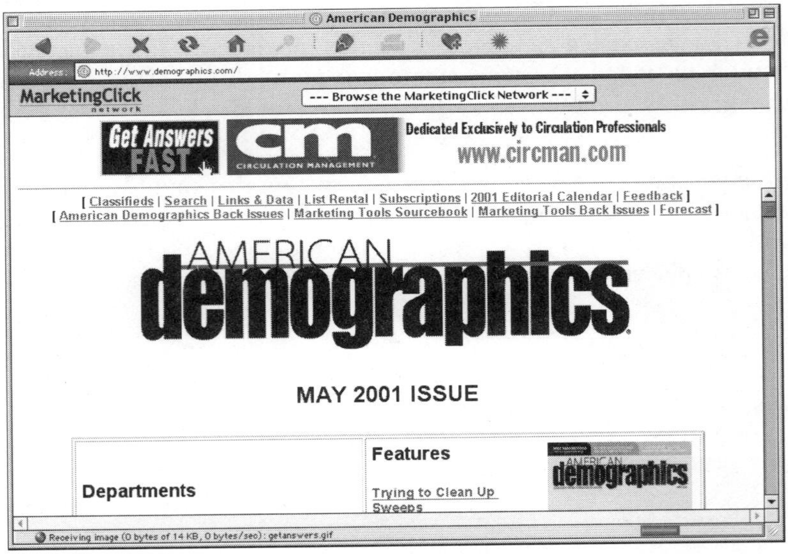

Figure 11.14
American Demographics presents well-researched information on trends in American lifestyles.

As you collect this information, however, keep in mind that many trends are transitory. You should trust your instincts when it comes to incorporating something trendy in your work.

Craft Shows

You can also use the Internet to research what craft shows are coming up in or near your area. The Art and Craft Shows database at **http://www.artandcraftshows.net/** (see Figure 11.15) lists more than 2,000 events in North America.

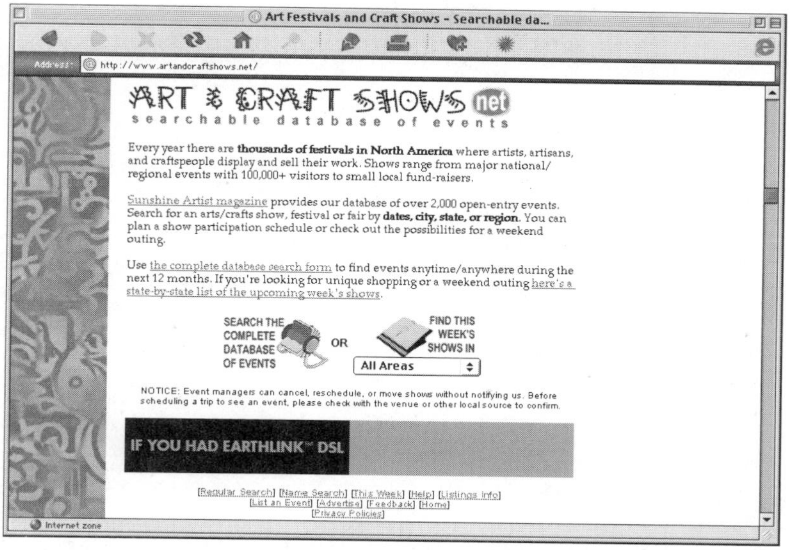

Figure 11.15
Art Festivals and Craft Shows allows you to search for events geographically and by date.

Section V Selling and Marketing Online

The shows are stored in a database that you can search by location and date (see Figure 11.16).

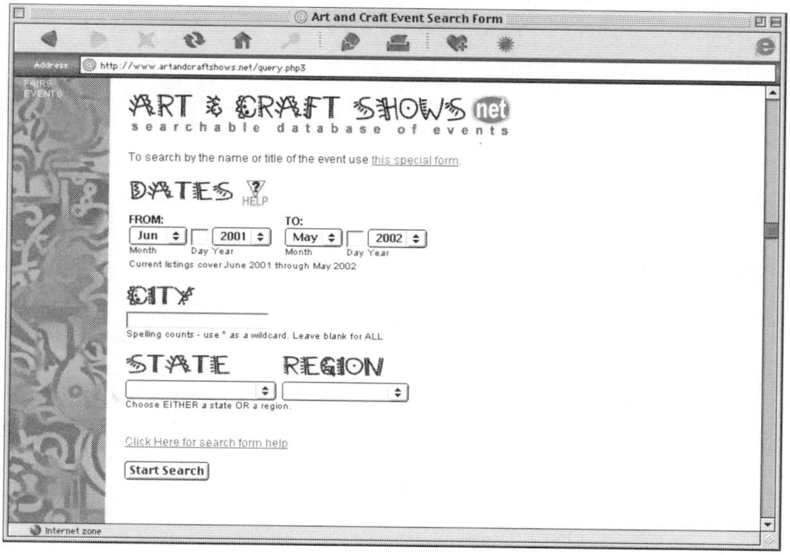

Figure 11.16
The search page at Art Festivals and Craft Shows.

The search results contain a lot of information about each show, represented by a series of icons (see Figure 11.17) illustrating the kind of merchandise sold at each show. This is useful information if you are trying to decide which show to attend.

Figure 11.17
Icons tell you what to expect at specific shows.

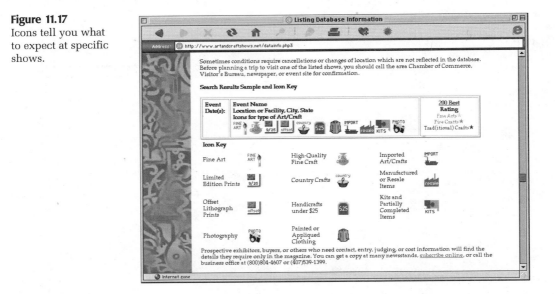

You can also find regional information on craft shows by looking for "craft shows" or "craft fairs" in your search engine and adding your state or province name. For example, I did a search on "craft shows" and "Ontario," and I came up with a list of shows on the Crafts Ontario site, **http://www.craftsontario.com/craftshows.htm** (see Figure 11.18).

Figure 11.18
Crafts Ontario is an
example of a site that
concentrates on a
specific region.

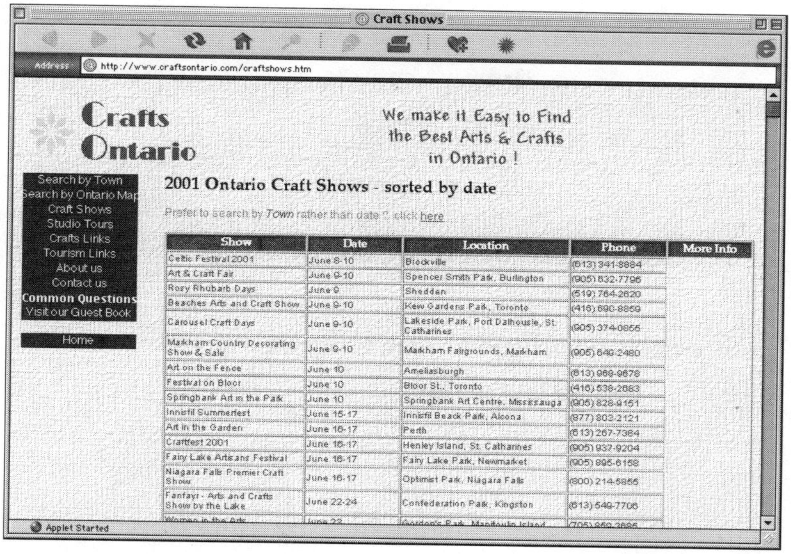

So, we've looked at online sources of information about the crafting business and collected some
ideas on what we can sell on the Internet. In the next chapter, we'll look at the different ways to
go about selling on the Internet.

12

How to Sell Online

This chapter is not about setting up a craft business, but rather how you can use the Internet in your business. Given some of the things you may already be doing in your craft business, we're going to look at how you can benefit from using the Internet.

Earlier, we talked about how you can interact with people all over the world. In the same way, the Internet can help expand your business by giving you visibility beyond your geographical boundaries—and also beyond the boundaries imposed by the clock, since your Web site is available twenty-four hours a day. In this chapter, we'll look at several different ways to sell on the Web.

Opportunities

In the craft industry, there are two kinds of things you might want to sell: products (such as finished crafts), craft supplies, or services (such as classes). Either way, you need to have a place online to showcase your wares and allow people to place orders.

One of the first things you might want to do is to investigate some crafting business Web sites to see how they use the Web. Use your search engine to look for sites selling products similar to the ones you want to sell. You'll find that selling opportunities on the Internet mirror those in the real world. You can sell at craft shows, take out classified ads, open your own store, rent a store in a shopping mall, put your crafts in a consignment shop, rent space in a crafter's co-op, and so on.

You have probably seen or heard the term "e-commerce." This simply refers to buying and selling electronically. There are several ways to do e-commerce, and we'll look at them in greater detail in the remainder of this chapter:

▶ You can have a simple "brochure" Web site, which is pretty much what it sounds like—a few Web pages that describe your business, along with contact information.

▶ You can have a Web site with an order form that people print out and either mail or fax to you.

▶ You can have a shopping site that includes a secure form that accepts credit card information and sends it to you in a secure manner. Note that this requires you to have a merchant account that allows you to process credit card payments.

▶ You can also have a shopping cart system where the credit card is processed by a third party.

▶ Finally, if you have a large business, you can have a full-fledged e-commerce site, which includes not only a shopping cart and credit card ordering, but also a connection to a database for catalogue and inventory purposes, and personalization. This level of functionality is beyond the scope of this book, though.

You should use your own online shopping experience to evaluate e-commerce opportunities. Remember all those things you should look for when you are shopping that we talked about in Chapter 9? Well, these are all the things you should provide to your customers. Be a shopper before trying to be a seller, and you can learn a lot about what your customers will expect (as well as what they don't like or feel comfortable with).

INTERVIEW

An Interview with Phyllis Tilford

Phyllis Tilford is a Certified Decorative Artist. She is a designer, teacher, frequent contributor to decorative painting magazines, distributor of the famous "Phylbert" brush, and author of six books and hundreds of pattern packets. She sells her books and patterns on her Web site, http://www.tolemill.com/ (see Figure 12.1).

Q: How long have you been selling your books and patterns on the Internet?

Six years.

Q: What made you decide to sell online?

I had joined an Internet painter's mailing list, and the owners of the list offered this to designers and businesses that were members at a fairly reasonable rate.

Q: How did you choose among the various ways to sell online?

I wanted someone that would do my "thinking" for me, as I was really computer illiterate. They offered basically three different ways of doing it. Since my designs are many, and we sell wood as well, I chose the largest of the selections.

Q: Do you consider the Web site a valuable part of your business?

Well, yes and no. If I run specials, I can expect more orders. If I don't, they pretty much just slow down. I do think anyone serious about this as a business should have a Web site. Many people are still shy about ordering and giving credit card info over the Internet, but they are able to view and see the designs before purchasing them. This is especially good for painters that don't have access to shops and don't get to conventions.

Q: Do you have any advice for someone who is considering selling online?

Well, nothing is going to do anyone any good, if people don't know about it. This takes some time, but I do think joining a mailing list that is related to what you are trying to sell does help. While you are not usually allowed to advertise your business, every time you post to a list, people do see your Web site address.

I always include my Web site address on all my packets, books, catalogs, business cards—anything that my buying public will see has this information

Figure 12.1
The Tole Mill is Phyllis Tilford's Web site where she sells books, pattern packets, and her special brushes.

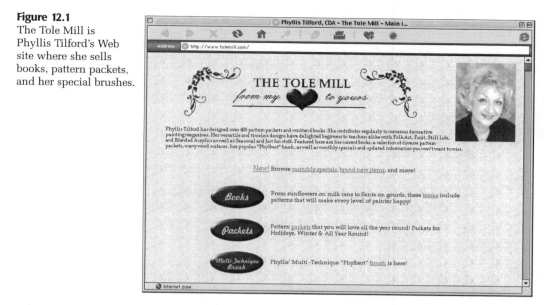

As with some of the other topics we covered, remember to ask for recommendations from fellow crafters you have met in discussion lists. Many will have gone through this already, and some will be willing to share their experiences.

Displaying Your Wares

There is one thing you are going to need no matter which venue you choose to sell your products: pictures. There are several ways to do this.

▶ You can take a photograph with a conventional camera, have it developed, and then use a scanner to bring the image into your computer.

▶ If the object is flat—for example, a greeting card, a small needlework piece, or a scrapbook page—you can put the object itself on the scanner without having to take a picture first.

▶ If you take a photograph with a regular camera, you can ask your film processor to have it developed onto a photo CD. You can then easily copy the images from the CD to your computer.

▶ If you have a digital camera, you can take a picture and then transfer the image directly into your computer from the camera.

▶ If you have the appropriate hardware in your computer, you can capture still images or video sequences from a video camera.

If you are going to be doing this a lot, you should invest in a digital camera or a scanner, or even both. A digital camera is good for convenience and portability, but unless you have an expensive one, you can get sharper detailed images with a conventional camera and scanner or photo CD. Try to take pictures in natural light, if possible, and have a neutral background that contrasts with your object. For myself, I purchased three pieces of fabric that I use for backgrounds when I photograph my pieces, one dark blue for light-color pieces and one gray and one beige for darker pieces.

NOTE

The format used to display photos on the Web is called JPEG (pronounced jay-peg), which stands for Joint Photographic Experts Group, the name of the committee that developed the format. This format is recognized by all Web browsers. If you are interested in technical information about the JPEG format, you can read the JPEG Frequently Asked Questions page at **http://www.faqs.org/faqs/jpeg-faq/**.

JPEG is the usual format for images from digital cameras or photo CDs. If you are using a scanner, you probably have a choice of several formats to save your pictures; make sure you pick JPEG.

There are several programs that can be used to edit your pictures, whether it's simple cropping or resizing or fixing the brightness or contrast. Two of the most popular are Adobe PhotoDeluxe or Paint Shop Pro. You'll find some Web links on the companion Web site where you can find these software packages. Many will let you download a trial version that you can use for a limited time at no charge. This allows you to try out several programs before you decide which is best for you.

In using the scanner, digital camera, or image editing software, you will sometimes be asked to specify the resolution of the image. The most common choices are 72 and 300 dots per inch (dpi). The main thing you need to remember is that 72 dpi is sufficient for an image that will be displayed on a computer screen; a 300 dpi image should be used if you are going to be printing the image, because printers are capable of finer resolution than computer screens.

Additionally, a larger image will load much more slowly, and many people have very little patience for Web pages that load slowly, so you want your images to be just big enough to show the item clearly.

Online Classifieds

Classified advertisements are an easy way to get started selling online. There are many sites that offer free classifieds ads, including Excite Classifieds at **http://classifieds.excite.com/** (see Figure 12.2).

Figure 12.2
Excite Classifieds offers free ads that include photos.

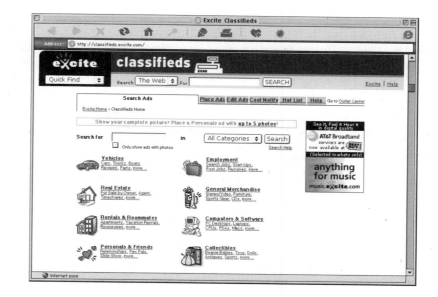

Unlike newspaper ads, online classifieds offer a potentially larger audience, plus searching capabilities to help visitors find what they are looking for. Another advantage is that some online ads can include a picture of the item for sale.

As a buyer—say, for example, I am looking for needlepoint items—I use the search box to look for the word "needlepoint" in all categories, and the search returns 139 items (see Figure 12.3). Listings can contain both text and an image of the item for sale.

Figure 12.3
Results from an Excite Classifieds search for "needlepoint".

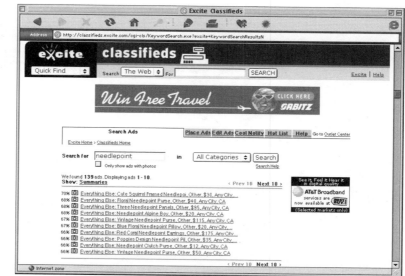

Section V Selling and Marketing Online

Once you are registered with the service, placing an ad is as simple as filling out a form. To begin, you click the "Place Ads" button. If you are not already registered with Excite Classifieds, you will have to register at this point. First, you choose the category and subcategory in which your ad will fit best. Then, as Figure 12.4 shows, you have to fill out a form, including the title, price, and description.

Figure 12.4
The first page of the
Excite Classifieds form

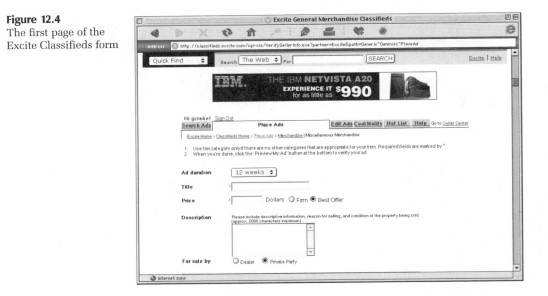

The second part of the form (see Figure 12.5) includes the payment methods you can accept and shipping information. This is also where you can include a photograph of the item for sale.

Figure 12.5
Page 2 of the Excite
Classifieds form.

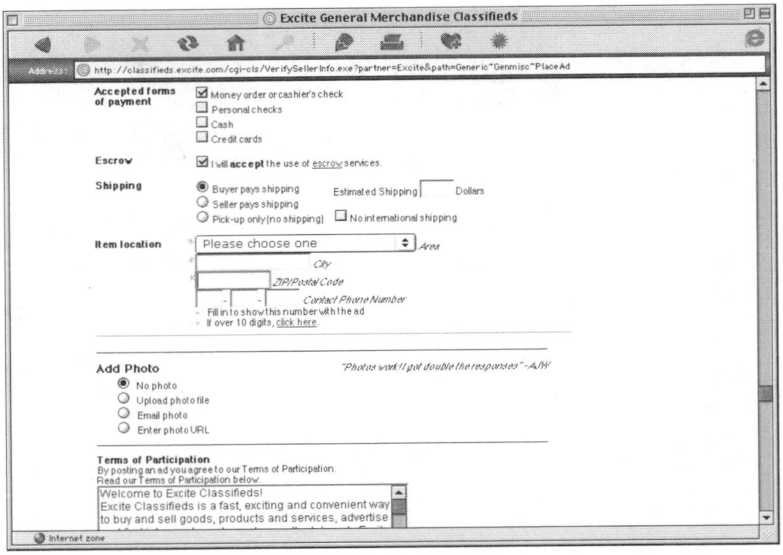

TIP

If you use any classified ad service, make sure you read the terms before you post an ad, so you will understand the rights and obligations of buyers, sellers, and the service itself. You also want to understand how the fees work, if there are any.

If someone is interested in your item, you will receive an e-mail so you can follow up and communicate with the potential buyer to answer questions or work out details of the sale.

There are other classified ad services, for example Yahoo! Classifieds at **http://classifieds.yahoo.com/**. These services work similarly, by having you fill out a form to submit your ad. One of the nice things about Yahoo! Classifieds is that there is a lot of helpful information displayed on the form.

Your Store in an Online Mall

Just like a brick-and-mortar shopping mall, an Internet mall is a collection of stores that are located together for shoppers' convenience. Yahoo! Store at **http://store.yahoo.com/** (see Figure 12.6) is an example of an online mall where you can open your very own store.

Figure 12.6
The Yahoo! Store
main page.

Again, like a real store, you have to pay rent for your presence in an Internet mall. In the case of Yahoo!, the monthly cost depends on how many items you want to sell in your store. You can try it out by setting up a store for ten days for free. Yahoo! also takes a small percentage if you choose to participate in Yahoo! shopping programs. There are many options for you to consider, so with any service you are considering, you should read all the information and make sure you understand the terms. You can usually find an e-mail address if you have any questions to which you can't find the answers.

To see an example of a Yahoo! Store, let's visit a Web site we saw earlier in Chapter 7, Craftideas.com (Figure 12.7).

Figure 12.7
The Craftideas.com
home page.

If you click "Shopping," you are taken to Craftideas.com's store (see Figure 12.8). This is an example of a Yahoo! store that illustrates some of the features available.

Figure 12.8
The Craftideas.com Store.

The store creation process includes many tools to make it easier for you. Figure 12.9 shows a sample store-management page; this page would be accessible only by you with your ID and password. You can see links for editing your site, checking your orders, statistics to tell you how many people are visiting your store, and other information.

Figure 12.9
A Yahoo! Store Management page.

Section V Selling and Marketing Online

On a store site like this, a lot of the work is done for you. This is an advantage because it saves you from worrying about a lot of details, but it can also be a disadvantage because you don't have the complete freedom that you would have with your own Web site. For example, there can be some limitations on what you can do with the look of the pages; also, you want to be careful about how the people who run the mall will treat your customers' personal information.

One good way to find out the pros and cons is to contact some of the existing store owners and ask how they find the service. You can visit some of the stores by starting at **http://shopping.yahoo.com/**.

TIP

If you decide to sign up with an online mall, be sure you understand the level of security provided by the mall, as well as the privacy policy for your customers.

There are other online services where you can set up a store, like Createastore at **http://www.createastore.com/** and Storehost at **http://www.storehost.com/**, and you can find more on the companion Web site. The features and fees can vary, so you want to shop around.

In addition to these general shopping malls, you might consider using an online mall that specializes in Arts and Crafts. One example is the Arts & Crafts Internet Mall at **http://www.artcraftmall.com/** (see Figure 12.10).

Figure 12.10
The Arts & Crafts
Internet Mall
home page.

Here are some of the things to find out before you sign up with an online mall:

- ▶ What are the fees and/or commissions?
- ▶ Can you find out some of their traffic statistics? And if you sign up with them, will they give you traffic statistics for your Web pages?
- ▶ What is their privacy policy with respect to your information and your customers' information?
- ▶ Do they provide secure credit-card transactions?
- ▶ How do you get your orders?

Auctions

You might not have thought of auctions as a way to sell your crafts, but many people have found that this is a great way to do just that.

This is an overview of what is involved in selling on eBay. For more information, the Help files available on the eBay site are very comprehensive. You can also communicate with other eBay users in the Community area.

NOTE

Since I am registered with eBay-Canada at **http://www.ebay.ca/**, this is what I will be using for the examples in this section. If you use the main eBay site at **http://www.ebay.com/**, the pages you see may look a little different.

Before You Start

Before you jump into selling on eBay, you want to do a little investigating. Spend a little time looking for items similar to yours to see how well they are doing. Search for a few items, and use the "watch this item" feature to keep track of them. Here is what you want to look for:

- ▶ How much the items end up selling for.
- ▶ How many bidders there were—this will give you an indication of the demand for this kind of item.
- ▶ What the description pages look like. Compare pages for items that did well with pages for items that did poorly.

Use this information to help you decide how to create your own ad.

Section V Selling and Marketing Online

Creating Your Listing

Start by clicking the Sell button at the top of the eBay page (see Figure 12.11).

Figure 12.11
eBay's main page—
the Sell button is on
the menu bar at the
top of the page.

In the first step (see Figure 12.12), you have to choose the category in which your item will be classified. This is important, because some buyers may only search within certain categories. If you're not sure which one to choose, search for similar items and see what category they are in. For this example, I choose "Everything Else."

Figure 12.12
Choosing a category—
the first step in creating
an eBay sales listing.

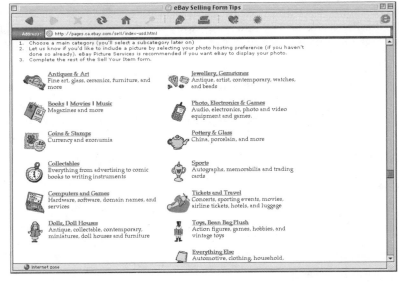

The next page is a long form where you enter all the information for your description page. Here are the main fields for you to fill out. The "Category" (see Figure 12.13) is actually where you choose a sub-category of the category you chose on the previous page. In this example, I chose "Crafts, Sewing" and then within that, "Tole Painting." Look carefully at all the categories to make sure you pick the best one for your item.

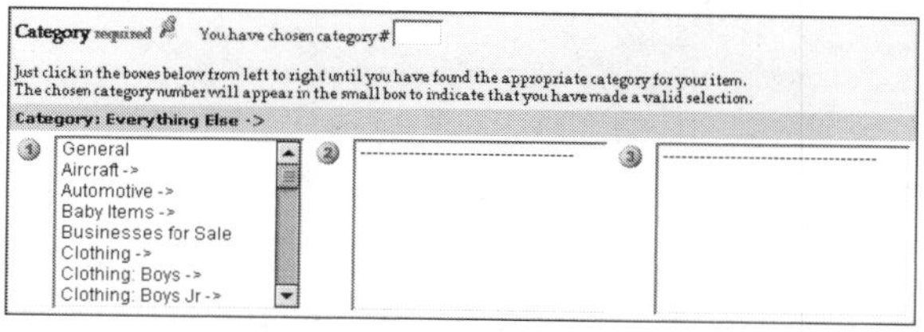

Figure 12.13
Choices in the Category box.

The "Title" and "Description" (see Figure 12.14) are vitally important to the success of your auction. First, check the tips pages—they contain some good information.

The title is limited to 45 characters, and how well you use those characters will determine how easily people can find your item. Think about what search words you might use if you were searching for such an item, then put together a title that contains as many of those words as you can manage. If you're having trouble, do a search and look at other titles and see what entices you to look at an item. Be very careful with your spelling, as people are less likely to find a word if it's misspelled.

The description is where you want to convince potential buyers that they want this item; try to anticipate what potential buyers would want to know about it. You can get inspiration from other descriptions on eBay or even from magazine ads or television commercials; pay attention to what kinds of things in an ad attract you to a product. Remember to include the dimensions of the object. Avoid too much hype, because this can definitely turn people off. Don't use ALL UPPERCASE LETTERS—this looks like you're shouting and it's difficult to read.

You can include some HTML formatting, if you want. HTML stands for HyperText Markup Language, and it's the formatting language used to create Web pages. There will be an introduction to HTML in Chapter 13; eBay also has an introduction to HTML on its tips page. You can use this to spice up the look of your description. Don't go overboard, though, especially with color and animation.

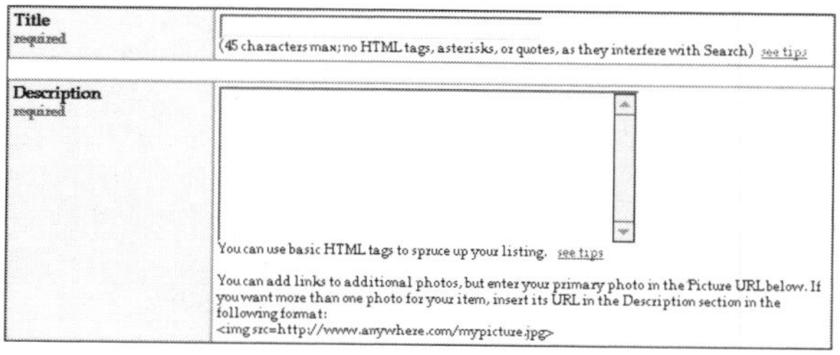

Figure 12.14
The Title and Description boxes—the next step in creating your listing.

Section V Selling and Marketing Online

Take care that the picture you put in your ad (see Figure 12.15) is a good-quality one that portrays your item in the best possible way. There are several options for you to get the picture into your ad on the eBay Web site; the simplest is to use eBay's own picture service, which is explained in detail if you click the Picture Services icon. If you want to enter your own Web address, click on "photo tutorial," just above this icon.

Figure 12.15
Adding your
photo—step 4.

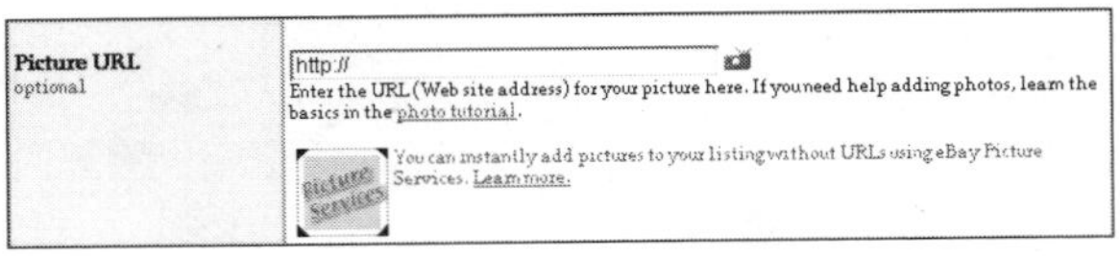

There is a screenshot showing a "Picture URL" field.

The Minimum Bid (see Figure 12.16) is the price at which you want your auction to begin; take care not to set this price too high or you might discourage potential bidders. The Auction Duration is either three, five, seven, or ten days. Consider making sure that your auction goes over a weekend; you could get a lot more people using the Internet then.

Figure 12.16
Set a minimum
bid here.

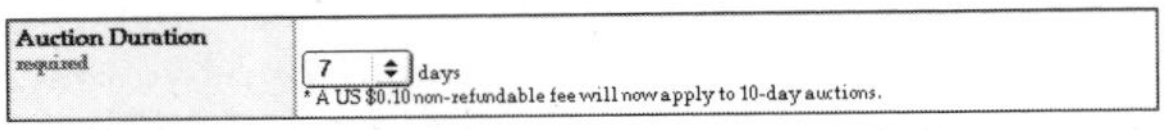

There is a screenshot showing an "Auction Duration" field.

There are several optional items, some which are free and others which incur an extra charge. One of the free options allows you to list your item in a second category (see Figure 12.17). This is an easy way to increase the exposure of your item.

Figure 12.17
You can list your item
in more than one
category if you wish.

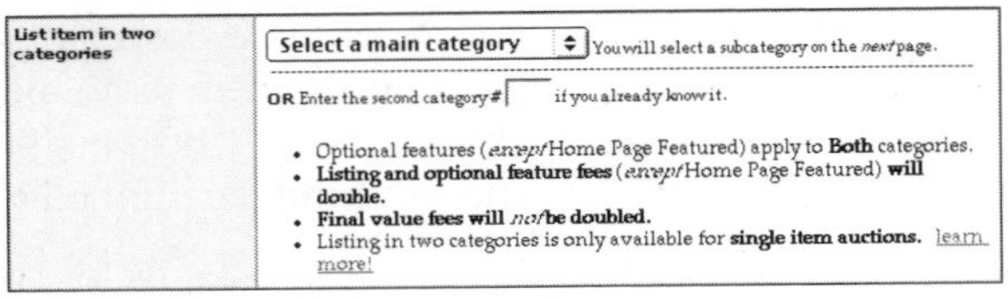

There is a screenshot showing "List item in two categories" options.

Another free option is a counter for your page (see Figure 12.18), which is a great feature for you to determine the popularity of your item.

Figure 12.18
See how many people
visit your listing!

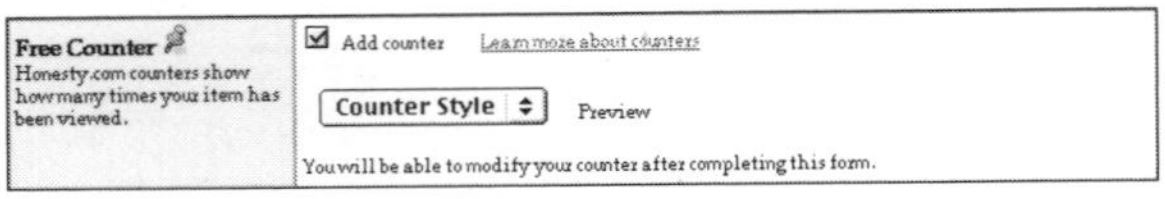

There is a screenshot showing a "Free Counter" option.

Finally, we get down to options related to the actual sale (see Figure 12.19), i.e., which payment methods you will accept and where you are willing to ship your item.

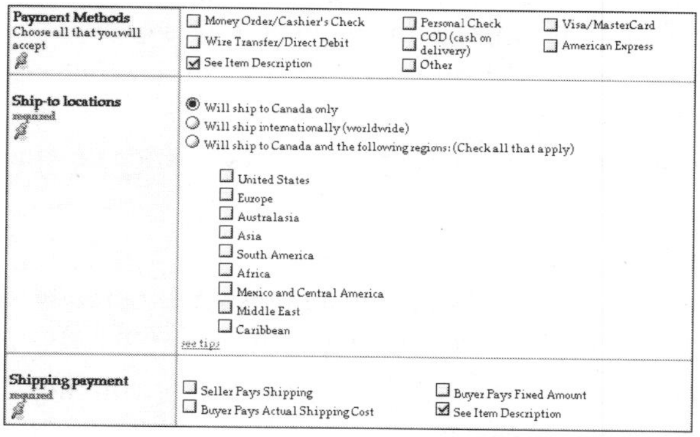

Figure 12.19
Getting down to
business—deciding
how to accept payment
and where to ship.

It's important for you to fill out this form carefully and provide the best information possible to potential bidders.

If you need help, click "Help" at the top of the page, then "seller guide," then "Boards." There are several discussion groups (see Figure 12.20) where you can ask questions.

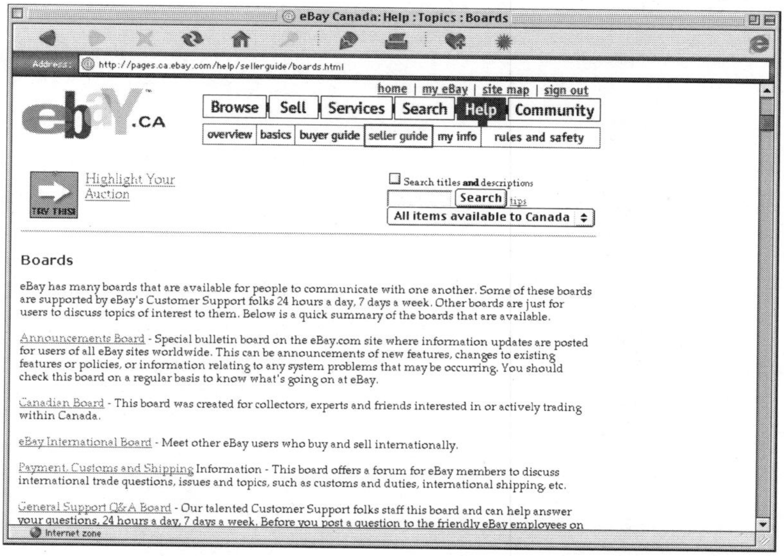

Figure 12.20
You can get help
from other sellers
on the eBay
Discussion Boards.

How Much Does It Cost?

On eBay, there is no fee for the buyer, but there is for the seller. There is an initial fee called the "Insertion Fee" for listing your item for auction. There are also fees for additional options, like a bold listing, where your title appears in bold text in lists or advertising on the eBay front page. Finally, there is a fee charged if your item sells successfully; this is a percentage of the selling price.

You can find the complete details in the "Help for Sellers" section on eBay.

During and After the Auction

During the auction, check your e-mail frequently and respond promptly to any questions from potential buyers. Always include the item title and number in any correspondence.

Once the auction is over, the first thing to do is to get in touch with the winning bidder by e-mail and work out the details for payment and shipping. In Chapter 10, we talked about the "feedback" that people on eBay can leave each other after a transaction; as soon as you find out who the winning bidder is, you can look up their feedback to see what other people have had to say about them.

After the whole transaction is over, you can leave feedback for the buyer, and the buyer may leave feedback about you as well. Feedback is very important on eBay, because it is used by everyone to find out details about people they might do business with.

13

Creating Your Web Site

There are many steps involved in creating and maintaining a Web site. In this chapter, we will talk about creating Web pages and getting them on the Web for the whole world to see.

A complete tutorial is beyond the scope of this book. What I hope you will get out of this chapter is an understanding of what is involved and a knowledge of the terminology, so that you can go on to the next step. Whether you decide to work on your own Web site or hire someone to do it for you, you will have a basic understanding of the process and of the possibilities.

NOTE

Throughout this chapter, I will be focusing on business Web sites; if you are creating a simpler personal site, you can still use a lot of the information. Just ignore the items that are business or shopping specific.

A Home for Your Site

Before you start, you need to consider where your Web site will reside. A Web server or host is a computer where Web sites are stored on the Internet. A hosting service is a company that runs one or more servers and sells space on them for people to store their Web site. In this section, we'll look at hosting options.

Section V Selling and Marketing Online

Free Sites

There are a lot of sites that offer you a "free" Web site. In exchange for giving you space for your Web pages, the service displays advertisements, and these advertisements supply varying levels of annoyance for the visitors to your Web site. Some ads are displayed as banners at the top of every one of your pages, others pop up (or pop under) in separate windows—sometimes more than one, so that visitors have to wade through all the windows to find the original page they wanted to see.

The first place you should look is your own Internet service provider (ISP). Most ISPs provide you with some Web space as part of your Internet account; it's not necessarily a lot of space, but it can be adequate for a small Web site, and it's a great place for you to experiment with Web development, if you choose to learn how to do it yourself. There are limitations, though. This Web space is not usually intended for commercial use, so it will not provide you with the things you need for a full-fledged e-commerce site. On the other hand, if you're a hobby crafter and you just want a place to display your creations for the world to see, this is perfect. Also, if you have a small business and you don't plan to sell on your own Web site, you can create a small Web site simply for promotional purposes. This is better than other "free" sites because you don't have to put up with advertising on your pages.

Now, these free sites are great for personal Web pages, and they are also a wonderful way for you to experiment with creating Web pages with no upfront cost. Some of them even have automated tools to help you create your pages. But if you want to establish a business presence and be taken seriously, you should consider alternatives. As a matter of fact, some of these free sites do not allow commercial ventures, and they will not usually allow you to have your own URL.

Finding a Host

A Web hosting service is a service that will sell you a place on the Web for you to put your Web site. In addition to hosting, many companies will offer to design the site for you and then promote it on the Web. There are various costs for these options, so you have to consider how much money you want to spend on the site and how much time you want to devote to developing and maintaining the site yourself.

The advantage of a hosting service over a free service is in what they offer, like your own domain name (that is, your own URL, such as www.yourbusinessname.com), a shopping cart with credit card ordering, detailed statistics on visitors to the sites, and more.

There are literally thousands of hosting services out there, and crafters will have a wide range of needs, so instead of talking about a service in particular, I will show you how to find hosting services and how to choose.

If you're serious about e-commerce, you have a wide range of options. Ask for recommendations from other crafters on discussion lists; many of them will have gone through this already and can give you useful advice.

If you're on your own looking for a hosting service, your first stop should be one of the sites that lists and reviews hosting services; there are a few listed on the companion Web site. For example, let's look at CNET's Web Host List, at **http://www.Webhostlist.com/** (see Figure 13.1).

Figure 13.1
CNET's Web Host List.

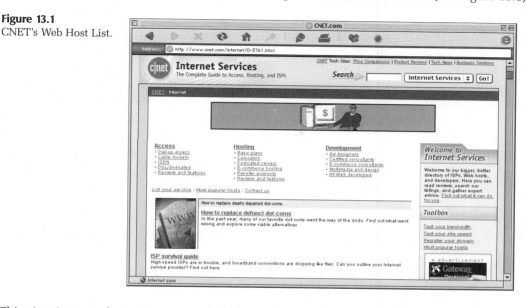

This site gives you lists of hosting services, ratings, and comparison charts. However you look at it, though, there is a lot to understand before you make a choice.

Your Options

As I mentioned, there are a variety of options, and you have to look at the trade-off between cost and features.

First, let's look at hosting and building the site.

► You can pay for hosting only and build your own Web site. This is a bit like leasing a piece of land and then designing and building your own house.

► You can use a service that provides hosting and pre-designed templates. You don't need to do any Web development yourself, just fill in some information in a form, pick out a template, and you're ready to go. This is like leasing some land and putting up a pre-fabricated house.

► You can buy a complete package where the hosting company will create a custom Web site built to your specifications. This is like leasing the land and hiring an architect to help you design the house, and then a construction crew to build it.

Section V Selling and Marketing Online

In order to choose from among those three alternatives, you need to decide how much you want to pay, how much control you want, and how much work you are willing to do yourself.

Now, let's look at the options available from hosting services and see what they mean.

> ▶ **Cost**—This will vary, of course, depending on the features you want. Once you understand the features you are looking for, you can look at comparison tables and get exactly the service you need for the best cost.

> ▶ **Development**—This tells you whether you need to know HTML, whether you need to use Web page development software, or whether you get only canned templates. Also, even if you want to develop the HTML pages yourself, you may want to know whether the service will provide extra custom programming (for example, special forms) for a fee as needed.

> ▶ **E-mail addresses**—The hosting service will provide you with a certain number of e-mail addresses for your use; unless your business is fairly large, you shouldn't need a large number of these.

> ▶ **Domain name**—Some hosting packages may include the registration fee for your domain name may perform the actual registration for you.

> ▶ **Additional features**—Look carefully at the list of additional features available, which may include forms, a guest book, a shopping cart, and secure ordering.

> ▶ **Backups**—You want to make sure that the service backs up your data regularly.

> ▶ **Statistics**—For a commercial site, it's important for you to know how many people are visiting. Look for a comprehensive set of statistics and, perhaps, charts that are easier to read than columns of numbers.

> ▶ **Limits**—This is one of the things that differentiates between packages with different costs. There may be limits on how many Web pages you can have, how many images, how many products for sale, or how much traffic the site generates. Of course, some of these things can be difficult to estimate at the start, so the thing to do might be to start with a more affordable site with lower limits and upgrade later if you need to.

> ▶ **Merchant account**—A merchant account is an account that allows you to accept credit cards. Some hosting services will require you to have your own merchant account, while others will provide the credit card processing for you as part of the service.

> ▶ **Privacy**—Check the privacy policy to find out how your information and your customers' information will be used.

> ▶ **Searching**—Not all sites will provide a searching feature. If you don't have too many different products, you don't really need searching anyway, but if you have a large catalogue, you may need this feature.

> ▶ **Promotion**—Once your site is built, you have to get people to visit it. (We will be talking about site promotion in Chapter 14.) Some services include some promotion as part of the package.

▶ **Examples**—Most services will provide you with links to sites that use their service. Check them out, see what they look like and what their features are like. You might even want to contact them to get their opinion of the service.

As with all the other kinds of services we discussed, it's very important for you to read the terms of service carefully so that you know precisely what you are getting, what your rights and obligations are, and the rights and obligations of the company providing the hosting service.

Getting Started

Planning your site before you jump in and create Web pages is very important. You want to think about the purpose of the site—for example, is it a brochure site used for promotion only, or is it an e-commerce site where you will be selling things? This will help you choose among the hosting options we looked at in Chapter 12.

The next step is to get your domain name, which will be the main part of your URL.

Your domain name will be the name of your site and would look like this:

yourbusinessname.com

The URL of your Web site will be the domain name with "www." in front of it. For example, my personal Web site is:

www.genevievecrabe.com

and the Web site I created for this book is

www.craftersinternet.com

If you have a personal or hobby Web site, it's not necessary to get a domain name. You can use the URL as provided by your ISP or hosting service, which may look something like this:

www.thehostingservice.com/yourname

If you are creating a business site, though, you should seriously consider getting your own domain name. The domain name, if you get one, should be as close as possible to your business name, although you may have to get creative with the naming if your business name is already taken.

Registering a domain name used to be a fairly involved process, but now it's very simple. You can start by looking for "domain registration" in your search engine and you will find many companies that will do it for you. There is a small annual fee to register a domain. Before you do that, though, if you have already selected a hosting service, you may find that it will do the registration for you, sometimes at a discount.

For example, the Web site yournamefree.com (see Figure 13.2) allows you to check if a domain already exists, and, if not, you can register it.

Section V Selling and Marketing Online

Figure 13.2
Yournamefree.com.

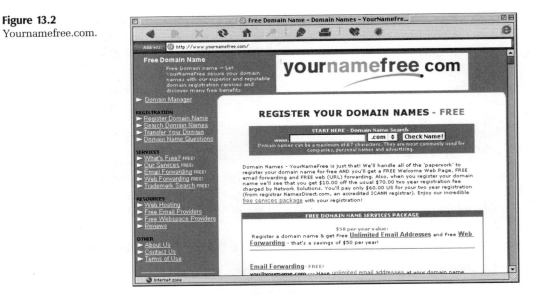

The registration isn't free, but this company does give you a discount and will forward your URL to an existing Web site if you wish. This means that even if you have a small Web site with your ISP—such as **www.thehostingservice.com/yourname**—you can still have your own domain name—**www.yourname.com**, for example—and this service will forward it automatically, so that when people type **www.yourname.com** in their browser, they will see your site.

One of the big advantages of having a domain name will be evident if you ever decide to move your site to a different hosting service. Say you didn't get a domain name, and your URL is currently:

www.thehostingservice.com/yourname

You have had this URL for a while, it's on your business cards and your stationery, you have registered with search engines, other Web sites are linking to this URL, and so on. Now, you have to move to another hosting service because the current one doesn't provide a feature you need. You now have a new URL:

www.someotherhostingservice.com/yourname

See all the things you are going to have to change?

On the other hand, if you have a domain name, it won't change if you change service providers. The only thing that changes is where the URL is forwarded to. Practically no work at all, and visitors to your site rarely will know anything changed at all.

Design Your Site

This is the stage in which you plan what your Web site is going to look like and what information it will contain.

Start by looking at a variety of Web sites. Get a feel for how they use the graphical elements; stop and consider your reaction to the look. Study how information is organized, how easy (or not so easy) it is for you to get around and find what you are looking for. You will begin to get a feel for the design of Web pages.

Also remember that you can learn from bad Web pages as well as good ones. Pay a visit to Web Pages That Suck at **http://www.Webpagesthatsuck.com/**—"Where you learn good Web design by looking at bad Web design" (see Figure 13.3).

Figure 13.3
Web Pages That Suck shows you examples of what not to do.

Visual Identity

If you are developing a personal page or a hobby site, you don't have to think in these formal terms, but in business, the graphics that you use on your Web site will reflect the identity and the image of your business. For example, if you are a decorative painter and you create items with a country theme, you probably don't want Web pages that look like chrome and neon. You want something that fits in with your products and your business image.

If you have the skills, you can design these graphics yourself, or you can hire a professional graphics designer to develop a visual identity for your business. You can also used pre-designed templates if you wish, but you run the risk of having your Web site resemble many others.

There are three types of visual elements that are used on a Web site:

▶ **The user interface elements**—These are the elements that are related to using the site, like titles and buttons.

▶ **Content elements**—These are pictures of the items you are showing or selling.

▶ **Eye candy**—These are elements that are used purely for decoration.

The user interface elements, if they are done right, will make it very clear where you are on the site, where you can go, and what you have to do to get there. Buttons should be clearly labeled, and if you want to use icons (pictures) instead of words on the buttons, use pictures that are easy to recognize.

Figure 13.4 shows some samples of button designs that might be used for a crafting site; the design elements include flowers, paint, wood, and fabric.

Figure 13.4
Buttons can be designed in a variety of shapes and text styles.

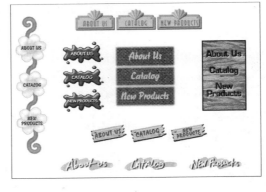

You should choose a design that's simple, straightforward, and related to your business.

Content

You need to determine what information is going to be provided by your Web site and how it is organized. If you're not sure what to include in these various elements, try visiting other Web sites to see what they have done.

To start with, you should have information about you and your company:

▶ The **About Us** page is where potential customers will expect to find out who they are dealing with. You can include some general information about your company, your mission statement if you have one, and whatever else you think you would like to know about a company before you order from them.

▶ A **Frequently Asked Questions** (FAQ) page can be very useful. In the beginning, you may not be sure what to put there, but after your Web site has been out there for a while, you will find that you get some of the same questions by e-mail from your visitors. These are the topics you can put in your FAQ.

▶ You should put a **Copyright** notice at the bottom of every page, if only to remind people that they mustn't copy your images or text.

▶ Make your **privacy policy** very clear and easy to find. People are becoming more privacy conscious these days, and they will want to know how you will treat the information you get from them.

Information about your products:

▶ Provide good **descriptions** of items for sale.

▶ You should have clear **pictures** of all the items for sale. Refer to Chapter 12 for some tips on taking pictures.

▶ Have a **What's New** page so that frequent visitors can quickly see what has been added recently. Be sure to update this page regularly.

Ordering information:

▶ If you have a **shopping cart**, it should be easy for customers to add and remove items and review the contents.

▶ Even if you have a shopping cart, you should consider providing a **printable order form**; this would be a simple Web page that people can print out and mail or fax. This provides an alternative to credit cards for people who don't feel comfortable using them online.

▶ After an order is placed, make sure there is an **e-mail confirmation** that the customer can reply to for customer service. If possible, provide a link to the shipper's Web site where they can track their order.

▶ Have a **Customer Service** page where people can find information and send an e-mail if they have a question.

▶ Explain the **shipping options** clearly, especially if you ship to other countries.

▶ Your **return policy** should also be spelled out.

In addition to selling stuff, you should provide a few extras that will give people a reason to come back. Here are a few ideas—I'm sure you can think of more:

▶ If you sell books, patterns, or supplies, you might have a page of crafting **tips**. Make sure to add to it regularly to keep the content fresh.

▶ Have an **e-mail newsletter** for your customers; you can have a simple form where people can enter their e-mail address to subscribe. The newsletter can contain news about the site, specials, etc.

▶ Everyone likes to get **something for free**. If you sell pattern packets, for example, you could offer a free one with someone's first order or even a free downloadable one for anyone who visits the Web site.

▶ **Contests** are another way to give away stuff, and regularly scheduled contests are a great way to get people to come back for a visit.

▶ You can have **specials** and advertise them in your e-mail newsletter.

Section V Selling and Marketing Online

An important step in the design is planning how the information is organized. You can represent this in the form of a flowchart (see Figure 13.5).

Figure 13.5
A flowchart can help you visualize the way your Web site is put together.

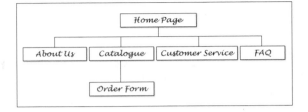

This sample flowchart is very simple, but it should give you the idea. You want to show all the different pages on the site (represented by boxes) and the links between (represented by lines).

You can even include a page on the site showing this flowchart (called a site map), where people can click one of the boxes and go directly to that page.

Ease of Use

A very important part of Web design involves usability—making your Web site easy to use. Study other Web sites and see if you can figure out the kinds of things that make one easy to use and another one difficult. People appreciate a Web site that is easy to navigate and where things are easy to find.

Here are a few simple guidelines:

▶ Your design should be consistent throughout all pages.

▶ Buttons and links should appear in the same place on each page.

▶ Keep the background light so that it doesn't interfere with the text.

▶ Put important content in the top part of the page so that people can see it without scrolling.

▶ Avoid pages that are long and require lots of scrolling.

▶ People should always be able to tell where they are.

▶ There should never be any dead ends (pages with no links on them).

▶ You may have seen some sites that start with a "splash page," a first page with a large graphic or an animation where you have to click "Enter" to go to the main page. Having a page like this can lead to user aggravation, especially with those who are on a slow connection.

▶ Keep your graphics small, and watch out for unnecessary design elements. If you want to include larger pictures of your items for sale, start with a thumbnail image in your catalogue and let users click the thumbnail if they want to see the larger picture.

▶ Never use underlined text. Since the beginning of the Web, underlined text has been associated with Web links, so if you underline a piece of text that is not a link, you will confuse your visitors.

▶ Spell check and proofread all your text more than once.

▶ Avoid "Under Construction" pages. If the content isn't there yet, leave the page out.

▶ Avoid background sounds or music. Some people may visit your site from their office and would prefer to be discreet. The sounds and music also slow down the loading time of your page, especially for people who have slower Internet connections.

If you want to learn about how to make a Web site easy to use, one of the best sources of information is the Usable Web at **http://usableWeb.com/** (see Figure 13.6).

Figure 13.6
The Usable Web is
a good resource for
design information.

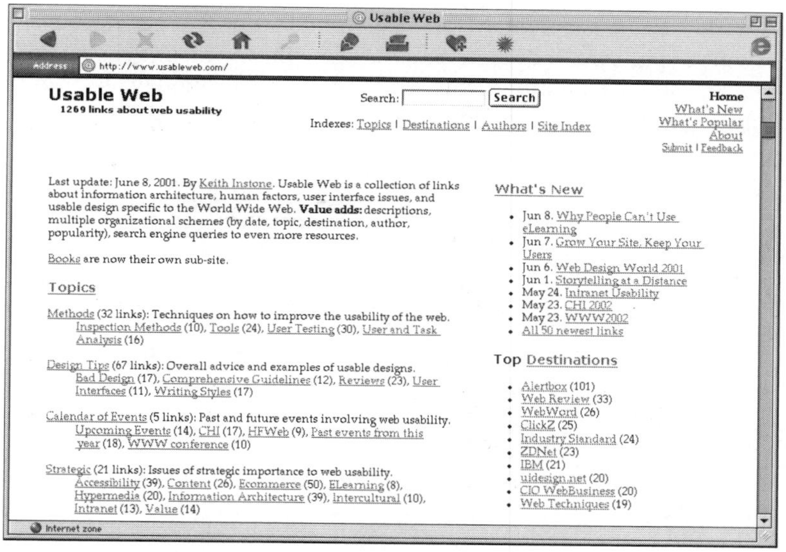

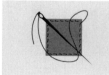

TIP
It is generally considered that one of the best books on the subject is *Designing Web Usability: The Practice of Simplicity* by Jakob Nielsen (New Riders Publishing, 1999, ISBN 156205810X).

Customer Service

Customer service is vitally important to any business, and it must be well represented on your Web site. There are many ways you can help your customers:

▶ Provide an e-mail address for people to ask questions and monitor this e-mail account regularly so that you can reply promptly.

▶ Many hosting services will provide you with "auto-responders." These are automated messages that are sent in reply to every message received at a particular e-mail address. Use auto-responders temporarily if you are away and cannot reply to e-mails in a timely fashion.

    ▶ Provide a form for people to give you feedback either about your products or about the Web site itself. If you get some good testimonials, you can ask for permission to quote from testimonials on the Web site.

    ▶ You can help your customers in another way, by giving them links to Web sites that contain useful resources for them. For example, if you sell needlecraft patterns, you could provide links to sites with needlecraft tips, related discussion groups, and sites that sell the supplies they will need.

Alternatives to Credit Cards

There are alternative payment systems you might want to consider, for example, PayPal at **http://www.paypal.com/** (see Figure 13.7). This allows you to register once with your credit card on the PayPal service, and then you can send or receive money electronically (through your credit card). You can even send money to someone who doesn't have a PayPal account.

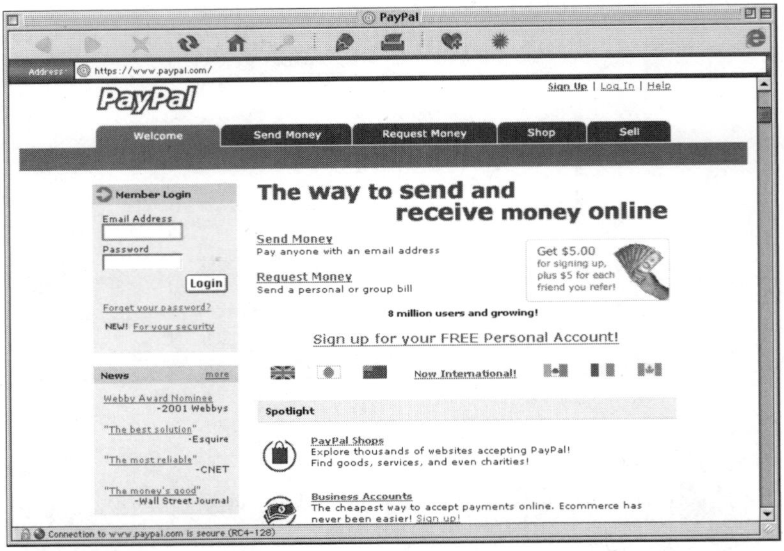

Figure 13.7
PayPal lets you
send and receive
payments through
your credit card.

This can be a great way to perform money transactions on your Web site.

Whichever method you use, read the terms carefully and make sure you understand them.

Develop Your Site

This section will give you a quick overview of what is involved in actually building your Web site after you've worked out the design concept and decided what elements you want to include.

HTML Basics

HTML stands for HyperText Markup Language. This consists of codes that are embedded in a text file to tell a Web browser what to display and how to display it.

In HTML, text is surrounded by tags that define the formatting. Most tags come in pairs; the opening tag looks like this <tag> and the closing tag is the same with the addition of the slash </tag>. Almost all tags have an opening and closing tag; this is important to remember, especially if you are writing your own HTML rather than using a program that creates it for you.

The file is the <html> tag, and the end is </html>. These tags simply tell the browser that this is an HTML file. The <head> tag defines the header portion of the page, and the <title> tag is where you define the page title that will appear in the title bar of the window. The <body> tag encloses all the content of the page. In the following example, the body is just one line of text. Included in the <body> tag is a modifier that tells the browser to display a white background.

There are many HTML tags. Table 13.1 lists the basic ones that I will introduce here.

Table 13.1
Basic HTML Tags

a	inserts the URL of a page to make a link
b	used to make bold text
body	encloses the main body section of the page
br	inserts a line break, without a blank line *
center	used to center text and images
font	used to specify text attributes: font, size, color
hn	heading (n = 1 to 6)
head	encloses the head section of the page
hr	inserts a horizontal line *
html	encloses the whole HTML page
i	used to make italic text
img	used to insert an image *
p	used to enclose a paragraph; paragraphs are separated from each other by a blank line
title	used to specify the title of the page that is displayed in the window title bar

* these tags do not have a corresponding closing tag

For starters, open a new text file. If you are using Windows, you can use Notepad, and if you're using a Macintosh, you can use SimpleText. Type this into the file:

```
<html>
<head>
<title>My Web Page</title>
</head>
<body bgcolor=white>
This is my first web page.
</body>
</html>
```

Save this file, call it mypage.html, and remember where you saved it.

Now, in order to see this file in your browser, if you are using Windows, you should be able to simply double-click the file icon. On a Macintosh, open your Web browser, choose "Open File" from the File menu, locate the mypage.html file, and open it. You should get something like Figure 13.8.

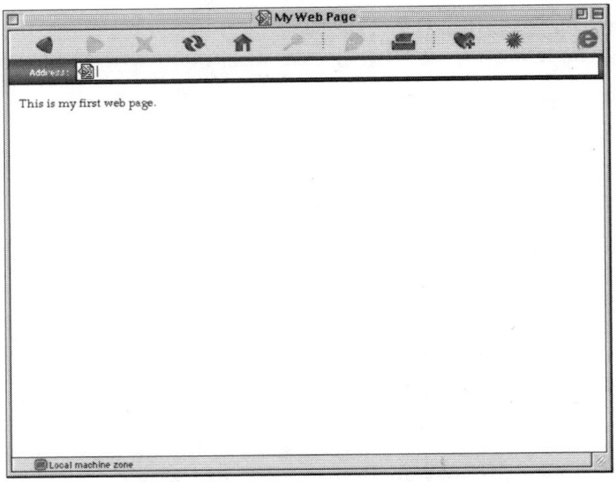

Figure 13.8
A simple Web page.

TIP
What you put in the <title> tag is what will appear in the Bookmarks (or Favorites) menu when people bookmark your site, so the title should be descriptive.

This is just about the simplest HTML page you can get. Now, let's introduce a few new tags:

```
<html>
<head>
<title>My Web Page</title>
</head>
<body bgcolor =white>

<h1>Welcome to my web site</h1>

<hr>

<p>This is my <b>first</b> web page.</p>

</body>
</html>
```

This Web page will look like Figure 13.9.

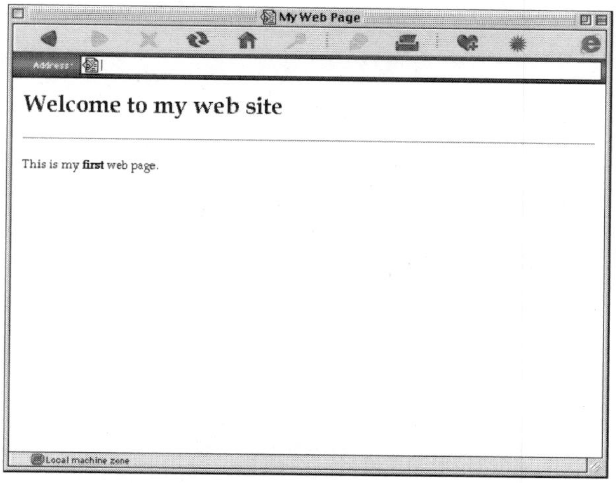

Figure 13.9
Our example page with
a headline and rule
added above the text.

The <h1> tag defines a level 1 heading; you can have other heading levels up to <h6> and each is a different text size, with level 1 being the largest. The <p> tag is the paragraph tag. If you don't use the paragraph tag, all the text you put in will run together even if you put returns; the <p> tag adds a blank line. The <hr> tag is a horizontal line ("hr" stands for Horizontal Rule), and the <b> tag is used to make text bold.

In the next step, get a JPEG image, perhaps one of your photos, and move it so it is in the same folder with the mypage.html file. Now try this (and remember to substitute the name of your picture file for "Flower.jpg").

```
<html>
<head>
<title>My Web Page</title>
</head>
<body bgcolor=white>

<h1>Welcome to my web site</h1>

<hr>

<center>

<p><font color=blue>This is an image:</font></p>

<img src="Flower.jpg" alt="Flower">

</center>

</body>
</html>
```

See the result in Figure 13.10.

Figure 13.10
We've successfully
added an image.

You can see that everything between <center> and </center> is centered on the page. And, with the use of the <font> tag, I have made the text blue. The <img> tag is used to display an image by giving its file name in the src (source file) attribute. The alt attribute of the <img> tag is a string of text that will be displayed instead of the image for those people who choose to browse with graphics turned off.

Now, let's see how to create Web links:

```
<html>
<head>
<title>My Web Page</title>
</head>
<body bgcolor=white>

<h1>Welcome to my web site</h1>

<hr>

<center>

<p>This is a link:</>

<p><a href="http://craftersinternet.com/"><b>Go to Crafter's Internet web site</b></a></p>

</center>

<hr>

<p>Please <a href="mailto:genevieve@craftersinternet.com">e-mail your comments</a>.</p>

</body>
</html>
```

See the result in Figure 13.11.

Figure 13.11
This sample page
contains a link
to another Web
page plus a link for
e-mailing me.

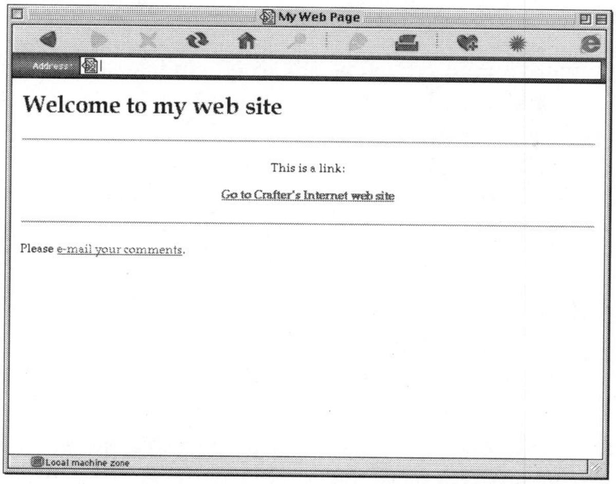

The <a> link ("a" stands for "anchor") is used to create links. In the case of links to Web pages, you write href followed by the URL in quotes, You can see in the result that the text I put in between the <a ...> and </a> tags becomes the link and is underlined.

TIP

When you type in the HTML tags, make sure to remember the closing tags, the ">" at the end of each tag, and all the quotes and equal signs.

Another kind of link is the e-mail link. Here, instead of a URL, you write "mailto:" followed by an e-mail address. Note that what happens when someone clicks on this link will depend on how their computer is set up. For some people, this will open an e-mail window in their browser, and for others it will go to their e-mail program.

This should give you a bit of an idea of how HTML works. If you are interested in exploring further, there are a lot of great books available on the subject.

TIP

If you are looking for an HTML reference, I recommend *HTML 4 for the World Wide Web: Visual QuickStart Guide* by Elizabeth Castro (Peachpit Press, 1999, ISBN 0201354934).

One thing you can do when you are browsing the Web is to take a peek at the HTML code behind the pages you are looking at. Use "View > Source" to see the HTML code for a page. How you do this may vary slightly between browsers, but look for an item called "Source" or "Page Source"; this is usually under View in the main menu bar (usually the View menu). This is a great way to learn HTML; also, if you see an interesting effect on a page, this allows you to peek under the hood to see how it's done and adapt the technique to your own pages.

Development Tools

There are some tools that can make your HTML writing easier than plodding along with Notepad or SimpleText, which are just plain text editors. These tools will provide some assistance in entering the tags and will display the tags in color in your source document so that you can distinguish them from the actual text content. My favorite tool on the Macintosh is BBEdit. There are some tools in Windows that will provide some of these functions, including HTMLed and HTML Editor.

NOTE

There are several software tools mentioned in this section. Look on the companion Web site for links where you can find these tools.

As interesting as HTML is, writing HTML from scratch isn't the way most people create Web pages nowadays. Although you can write simple Web pages directly in HTML, there are many software packages that let you develop your pages in a WYSIWYG fashion. WYSIWYG stands for What You See Is What You Get, and it means that instead of writing HTML code, you use something that looks more like a word processor, so that you see and edit your Web page in a window where it looks more like the way it will appear in the browser. In fact, if you use one of these tools, you never have to look at the HTML code unless you want to.

Here is an example. Figure 13.12 shows a small Web page as it appears in my browser.

Figure 13.12
Our example Web page as it appears in my browser.

Figure 13.13 shows the same Web page in BBEdit. You'll have to take my word for it that the HTML tags are in color.

Figure 13.13
The same Web page in BBEdit, showing the source code.

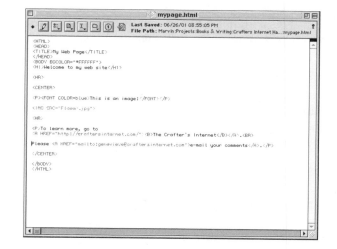

Figure 13.14 shows the same Web page in Netscape Composer, which is part of the Netscape Communicator package (and, therefore, free). As you can see, this looks just like the page in the browser (see Figure 13.12), except that this is the editing environment; you can see the tools at the top of the window.

Figure 13.14
The same Web page in
Netscape Composer.

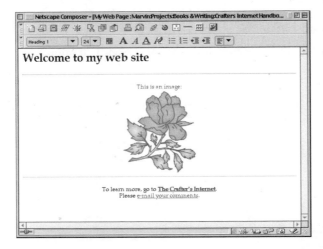

There are many other Web development software packages (see the companion web site for some links) available at a very wide price range. Which one you choose depends on how much of the Web development you want to do yourself. Many of these packages will allow you to download a free trial copy that will be fully functional for a limited time, usually thirty days. This allows you to try before you buy.

If you decide that you want to do some of this yourself, there are several affordable ways for you to get some training.

▶ There are a great number of books out there, and more coming out all the time. Check online bookstores for a full selection.

▶ You could look for some local classes, perhaps some continuing education classes at a high school or community college.

▶ There is also some interactive training available on the Internet. One site that offers affordable introductory classes is Learn2.com at **http://www.learn2.com/** (see Figure 13.15).

Figure 13.15
Learn2.com offers
training online.

You might not want to take on the whole job of creating your Web site from scratch, and indeed you could hire someone to do that. But if you can learn some of the basics, that might be enough for you to be able to make changes yourself, rather than bringing in the developer every time you need a small update.

Testing

Once your Web site is completed, it must be tested thoroughly before taking it live to make sure everything works as it should. Open the site in your browser, check all the links by clicking each one, and if you have a shopping cart, you need to ensure that everything there is working properly.

In addition to testing on your own computer with your own browser, you need to test on the other major platform—that is, if you are developing on a Macintosh, you should make sure everything works properly in a Windows Web browser, and vice versa. Similarly, you need to test using both major browsers, Netscape and Internet Explorer. You can do this yourself if you have access to more than one computer, or you can find friends who have different computers and use a different browser.

The minimum you should test is the current versions of Netscape and Internet Explorer (both free) in both Windows and Macintosh operating systems. You might also want to test with America Online and with a couple of earlier browser versions, because not everyone is using the latest.

User Testing

In the user interface design business, user testing is one of the most important parts of the process. Whenever someone designs a new product, it is given to people to try out—people who were not involved in the development of the product and who can approach it the same way as the consumers who will end up buying it.

It's the same for a Web site. Because of your involvement with the design and development, even if you're not doing all the work yourself, you're not the best judge of the usability of the Web site.

Before your site goes live on the Internet, bring in a few people who have never seen it before to try it out. Try to find people who are similar to those who make up your target audience, and sit them down in front of the computer with your Web site. Before they start, explain that they are not the ones being tested, it's your design, and that if they have trouble with something, it's not their fault, it's something you will have to fix in your design.

Now comes the hard part: You have to be quiet. Let them explore as if they were alone in their houses. Encourage them to talk out loud about what they're doing. This is difficult for some people, so you might consider having two people do this together, because they are more likely to talk to each other.

The information you will gather from this process will tell you how easy or difficult it is for people to find their way around the site, and you will get some useful insights.

Add-Ons

So you have your basic Web site where you're selling your craft items. Here are a few ideas for other things you can add to your site to make it more interesting and build interest in you as a crafter.

You could write a short book about your craft, filled with tips based on your experience. You could simply save this book in a computer file and make it available for download on your site for a small fee. One of the nice things about selling an electronic document is that you don't have to worry about shipping anything—the entire transaction is done over the Internet.

Have you ever thought about opening your own bookstore? Well, now you can. Some online bookstores like Barnes & Noble have an affiliate program (see Figure 13.16). Click **Build Your Own Bookstore** on the main page at **http://bn.com/**.

Figure 13.16
Barnes & Noble uses
its Affiliate Program
to encourage Web links
to its store.

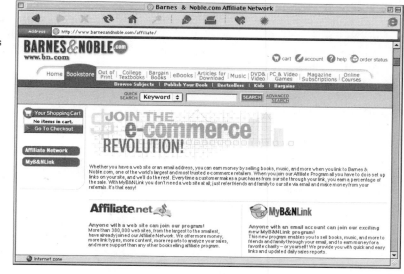

This program allows you to sell books on your Web site; the actual sale is handled by Barnes & Noble, and you get a small percentage. You can take advantage of a program like this to enhance your Web site by selling books that are related to your craft. If you are an author, you can sell your own books. Many commercial sites have affiliate programs.

Even some craft suppliers have an affiliate program, for example, ArtistsClub.com. For information on the program, go to **http://www.artistsclub.com/** and click the link **Affiliate Program** at the bottom of the page.

CafePress at **http://www.cafepress.com/** (see Figure 13.17) offers another kind of add-on to your site. Through CafePress, you can sell T-shirts, mugs, and mousepads with your own artwork. You can use a picture of your own artwork or your company logo; all you have to do is create a store on their site (no charge), upload the picture, and then provide a link on your Web site. See the CafePress Web site for more details.

Figure 13.17
CafePress enables you to sell items featuring your artwork.

At some point, you may want to get some feedback on your Web site or on your products. Many Web sites offer tools for creating interactive survey questionnaires. One example is Zoomerang, at **http://www.zoomerang.com/** (see Figure 13.18). There are more examples on the companion Web site.

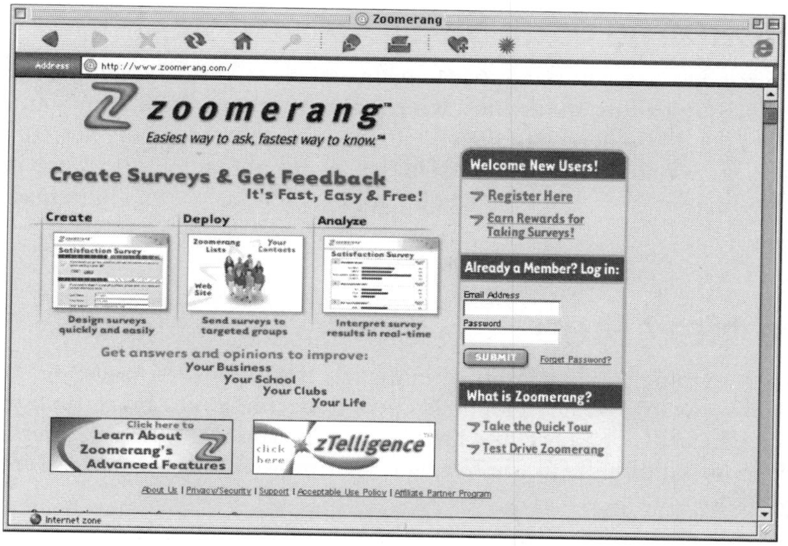

Figure 13.18
Zoomerang is a site
that helps you gather
feedback.

There is a simple point-and-click interface for creating a survey; you can see an example in Figure 13.19. Once you have created the survey on the Zoomerang site, the instructions will tell you how to link to it from your Web site.

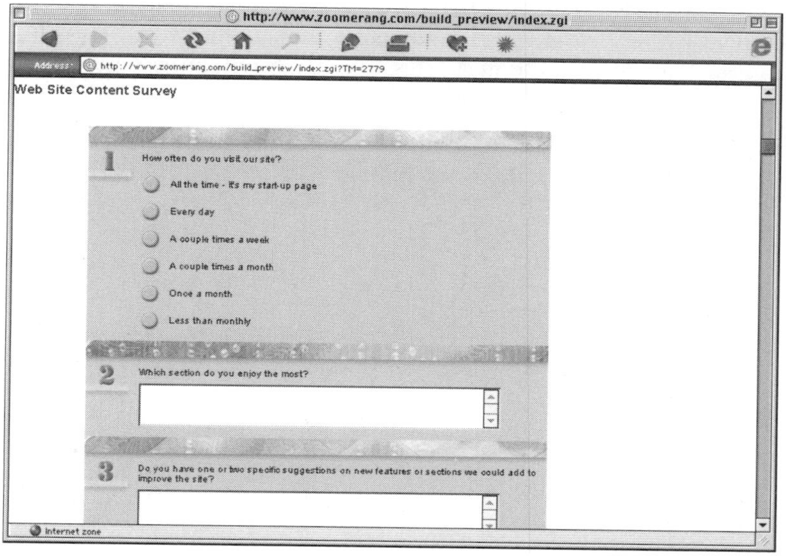

Figure 13.19
A sample
Zoomerang survey.

Uploading Your Site

Once your site is developed, it has to be installed on a Web server that is connected to the Internet by uploading all the files, which means copying them from your computer to the server. Exactly how this is done will depend on where your site is being hosted. If you hire someone to develop your Web site, they will usually take care of that for you. If you are doing it yourself, your hosting service will provide you with instructions on how to upload your files to their server.

The Next Step

Given everything you have learned in the last three chapters, you should now be better prepared to decide how to proceed. It all boils down to deciding how much time you want to spend learning the skills you need and how much time you want to spend working on your Web site. If it is more worthwhile to you to spend your time crafting, then you want to hire someone to do the work for you.

As I mentioned earlier, you can hire someone to design and implement the site; then you can maintain it yourself for small changes, going back to the designer for major updates such as design changes and significant catalogue updates. Or you can hire someone to do the graphic design and do the rest yourself.

Watch out for cut-rate developers, though. Simply learning HTML doesn't make someone a professional Web designer, just like learning the English language does not make someone a professional writer. Before you hire someone, look at their work. Does it look professional? Is it easy to use? You also want to make sure a designer will be responsive to your needs and, for example, not try to sell you a high-tech look when you want country.

So, now you have a Web site. How do you let people know about it so they will come and visit? That's what we'll look at in the next chapter.

14

Attracting Visitors to Your Web Site

Now that you have built your Web site, you need to develop a marketing strategy to get people to visit. This is called building, or increasing, traffic. In this chapter, we will examine several ways to accomplish that goal.

First of all, you need to make sure your site is ready for public viewing. If you haven't already, proofread and spell check all your pages; typos and grammatical errors leave a bad impression with visitors to your site. Also, check all your Web links to make sure they work. Links to other sites should be checked regularly to make sure those sites haven't changed, moved, or closed down.

We have already talked about getting your own domain name. While this is not necessary for a personal or hobby site, having a domain name for your business will give you a greater level of credibility, both with people and with search engines when you try to get listed.

I will be introducing many new terms in this chapter. There is a great resource on the Internet that you can use to find definitions of computer and Internet terms: **http://whatis.com/**.

Search Engines and Directories

In Chapter 3, we talked about how to find things using search engines and directories. In this section, we'll see how you get your own Web site listed so that other people can find you.

How Information is Collected

A search engine uses a program called a "crawler" or "spider" that scans through Web pages and indexes the words it finds, concentrating on the words that figure more prominently. So, for example, if the word "quilt" occurs several times on your home page, once your site is indexed, it should show up when someone does a search on the word "quilt."

The ranking that your site receives in the search results—how close it shows up to the top of the list—is determined differently by different search engines. Google, for example, will give you a high ranking based on how many other sites have linked to your site. Other search engines look at other criteria, including the words you use in your page titles, headings, and text close to the top of the page.

Search engines like Google at **http://www.google.com/about.html** (see Figure 14.1) will give you some information about how rankings are determined, as well as tips on submitting your site. We'll look at submissions a little later.

On the Search Engine Watch Web site, you will find a table that describes the way different search engines determine their rankings: **http://www.searchenginewatch.com/Webmasters/features.html**.

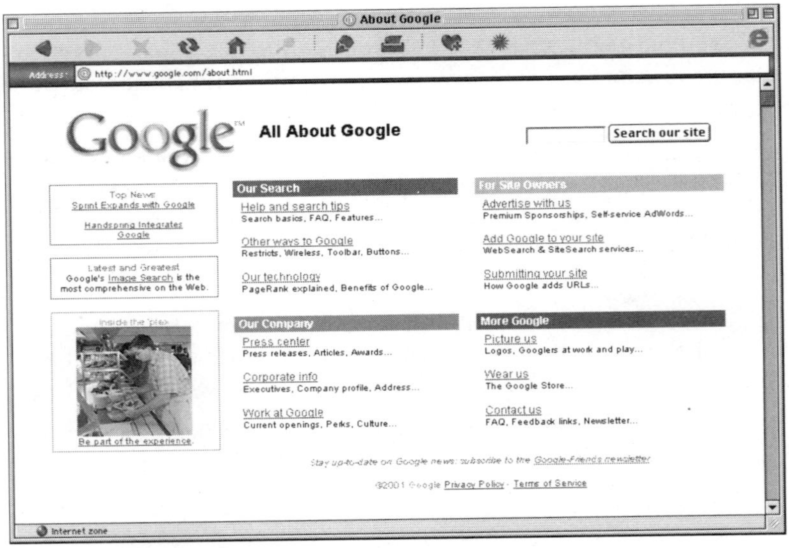

Figure 14.1
The Google "About" page is the gateway to learning how to be listed with this popular search engine.

Using HTML Tags

There are some things you can do in your HTML tags to help with your search engine rankings. If someone else is developing your site for you, ask whether they will optimize your site for search engines.

The <title> tag is very important. Choose your title carefully, because this is what will usually show up as the title in the search engine listing. You don't want something non-specific like "Welcome to my Home page." At the least, the title should contain the name of your business; you should also include a word or words that describe the business if that word is not already part of the business name.

Section V Selling and Marketing Online

Here's an example. Suppose you have a needlepoint shop called "Jane's Needlepoint Shop." You can use the name as is, since it already contains the word "needlepoint":

```
<title>Jane's Needlepoint Shop</title>
```

On the other hand, if the name is "Jane's Creations," then you want to add something like this, so that the word "needlepoint" appears in the title:

```
<title>Jane's Creations - Needlepoint Shop</title>
```

Another set of tags that is important are the heading tags <h1> to <h6>. The lower number heading tags are the most important headings, and the text they contain will be given greater prominence by the search engine.

Since the search engine indexes text on your page, it cannot read something that is represented by an image. This is why it's important to always include the alt attribute in your <img> tags (see Chapter 13 for more about alt tags).

An important set of tags used by the search engines are the <meta> tags. These are special tags you put in your home page, inside the <head> section. These are not displayed on the page, but they work behind the scenes to give information to search engines, Here is an example:

```
<meta name="description" content="Jane's Creations sells needlepoint kits and
supplies.">

<meta name="keywords" content="needlepoint, needlecraft, charted design,
needlework, petit point, stitching, canvas, gifts">
```

The first is the description, which should be kept under 200 characters in length. This is the description of your site that will be displayed by the search engine when your site shows up in search results. You should spend some time composing the best description you can come up with for your site.

The second is a list of keywords that will be included in the search engine's index. When someone enters one of these words in the search engine, your site should be one of the ones listed.

You should pick your keywords carefully. Think about how you use a search engine—what words would you use to search for a site like yours? List the keywords in order of importance, because some search engines have a limit on how many they will use. You want to have the most important ones at the beginning.

Check out competing Web sites to see how well they are ranked in search results, and use the View Source feature of your browser to see what keywords they use in their <meta> tags. Here are just a few examples of keywords you might want to use for various crafts; you can pick and choose which ones apply to your site, and I'm sure you can think of more keywords.

Table 14.1

Typical keywords at craft Web sites.

Craft	Sample Keywords
General Keywords	crafts, projects, gifts, giftware, hobby, hobbies, craft supplies, home accents, books
Decorative Painting	decorative painting, tole painting, acrylic painting, art, brushes, paint, folk art, medium, primitive, stencils, watercolor, faux finish, murals, trompe l'oeil, trompe l'oiel, artwork, fabric painting, wearable art, one stroke
Needlepoint	needlepoint, cross stitch, cross-stitch, crossstitch, embroidery
Cross-Stitch	needlecraft, crewel, charted design, needlework, petit point, stitching, canvas
Embroidery	stitchery, floss, latch hook, ribbon
Knitting, Crochet	knit, knitting, crochet, crocheting, yarn, wool, charted design, needle, hooks, intarsia
Sewing, Quilting	fabric, sewing, quilt, quilting, needles, patterns, stitching, thread, patches, squares, applique
Scrapbooking	scrapbooks, scrapbooking, journaling, rubber stamps, stamping, photos, scrapbook paper, albums, vellum, punch outs, memory albums, archiving, die cut
Other crafts	floral, candles, soap, mosaics, decoupage, woodworking, candlemaking, basketry, weaving

Note that you may want to include variations of the same words—and also common misspellings of some of your keywords. That way your site will be found even if the person searching misspells a search word.

Here is a summary of where the search engine will look for the important words to index your site:

▶ Your page title in the <title> tag

▶ Keywords in <meta> tags

▶ The headings

▶ The alt text in <img> tags

▶ Text close to the top of the page

Submitting Your Site

All search engines have a form where you can submit your Web site. Figure 14.2 shows the submission page for the Excite search engine. This submission is free, but it is for review only. Excite does not list all submissions. There are further options available for a fee, including a faster submission review and advertising.

Figure 14.2
The Excite submission page. Note that Excite does not guarantee your site will be included. Paying a fee shortens the time to be considered for inclusion.

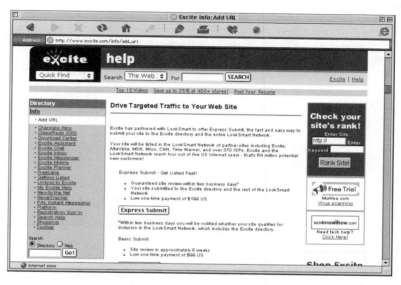

On some search engines, you can purchase advertising space, targeted to come up when certain keywords are used in a search. For example, Figure 14.3 shows a search on Google for "decorative painting." The ads on the right are the kind of ads that you can purchase.

Figure 14.3
The Google search results page displays paid advertisements at the right.

Section V Selling and Marketing Online

The advertising page at **http://www.google.com/ads/** (see Figure 14.4) explains various options for purchasing advertising space.

Figure 14.4
Google currently
provides two levels
of advertising.

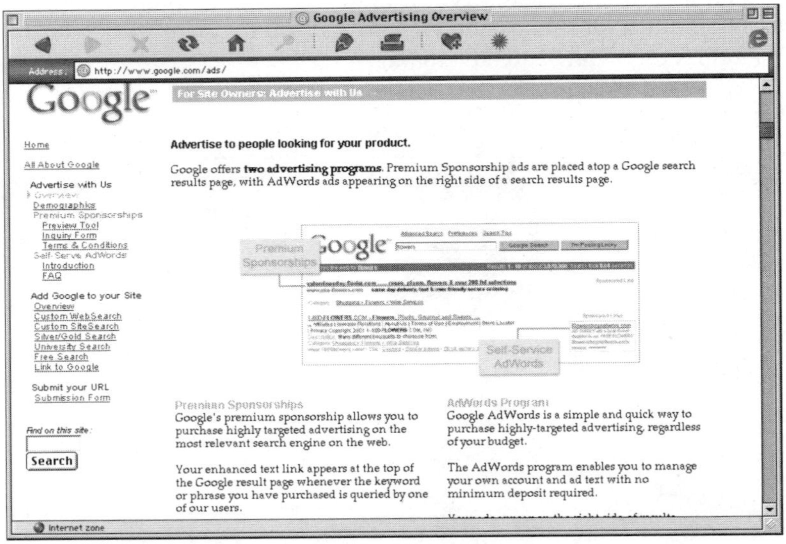

When you decide to start submitting your site to search engines, begin with the major ones like Alta Vista, Google, and Excite. Take your time and read the instructions provided by each one.

There is a lot to learn about submitting to search engines, and there are several Web sites that contain a wealth of information on the subject. The Search Engine Watch Web site at **http://www.searchenginewatch.com/** (see Figure 14.5) has a section on search engine submission tips. This includes an explanation of how search engines work and how they rank Web pages, plus search engine placement tips and how to use <meta> tags.

Figure 14.5
Search Engine Watch
offers information
on search engine
submissions.

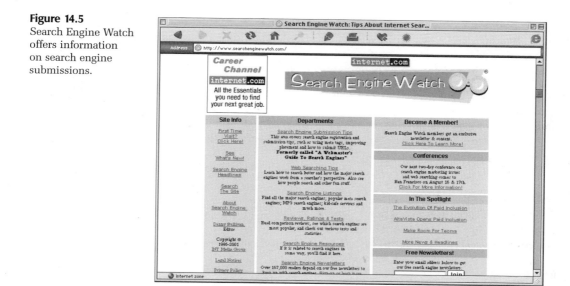

The information on Search Engine World, at **http://www.searchengineworld.com/** (see Figure 14.6), is more technical and includes in-depth information on search spiders and how they index your pages.

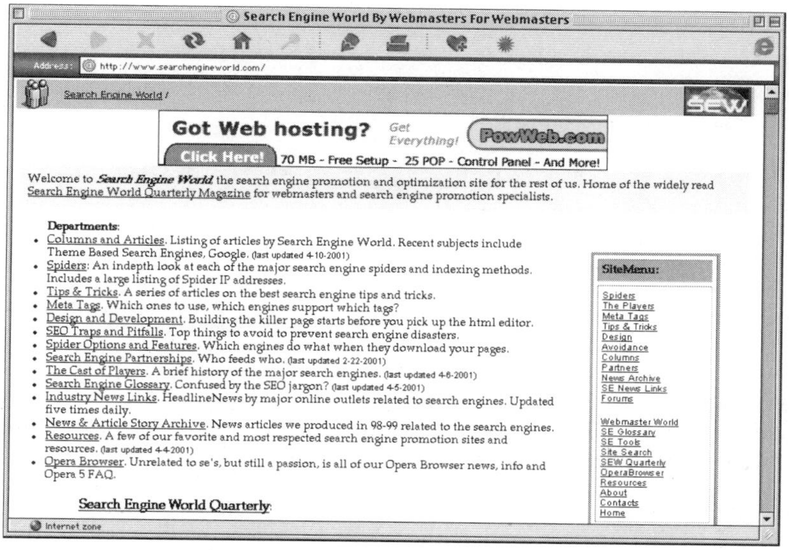

Figure 14.6
Search Engine
World provides more
technical information.

As you submit your site to search engines, keep a log of where and what you submitted. Go back periodically and check your presence and your ranking on those search engines. Note that some search engines require periodic resubmission; you can find information on this on Search Engine Watch at **http://www.searchenginewatch.com/**.

In addition to the standard search engines, you should consider submitting to country-specific or regional sites. For example, if your business is in Canada, you should submit your site to the Canadian versions of search engines like **http://altavista.ca/** and Canadian search engines like **http://canada.com/**. You should also submit your site to craft-specific sites such as **http://www.craftsolutions.com/**.

Submission Services

As you can see, submitting your site to search engines can be a complex and time-consuming process. If you don't want to do it all yourself, there are services that will submit your site for you. One such a service is Submit It!, at **http://submit-it.com/** (see Figure 14.7).

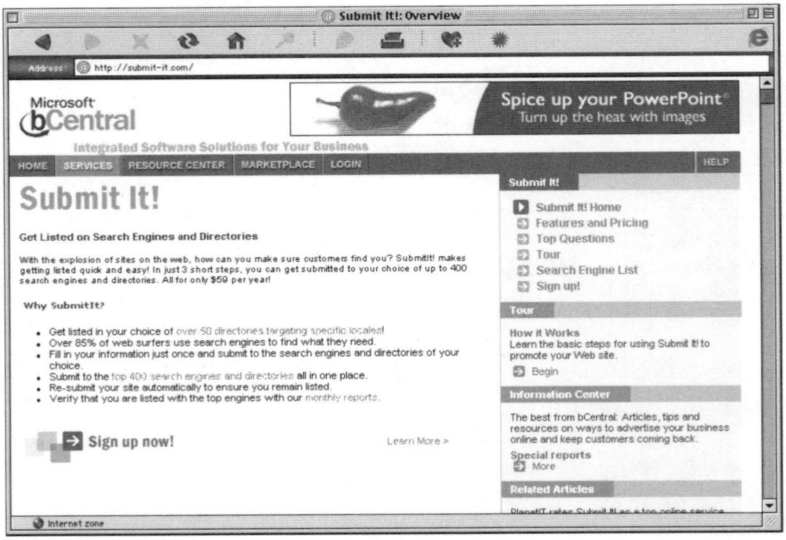

Figure 14.7
Submit It! will take over the chore of search engine submissions for you.

For a fee, this service will submit your site to a variety of search engines. It includes an analyzer that can help improve your <meta> tags and check your site for broken links. You also receive monthly reports on the submissions. Some of these services may even offer limited services for free.

You may find that using a service like this will save you a lot of time and effort, and this can be money well spent, depending on your situation. You can judge the results for yourself by checking how and where your site comes up in the search engines and then deciding whether you want to continue with the same service or sign up with another one.

You can find URLs to some additional submission services on the companion Web site.

Note that a service like this may not submit your site to the craft-specific sites, so you may have to do that yourself.

Directories

In Chapter 3, we looked at the differences between search engines like Google and directories like Yahoo!. There is also a big difference between them when it comes to submitting a site. Directory submissions are reviewed by people, as opposed to search engine submissions, which are handled automatically by software.

Also, directories tend to be very selective about which sites they accept, because they want to maintain a high quality for their users. This means that there is no guarantee of acceptance when you submit your site to an online directory. Yahoo! is certainly one of the most popular sites used by people to look for Web sites. Even if the chances of being listed are slim—because it's one of the more difficult places to get listed—it's worth a try.

You want to start by carefully examining the categories to determine where your site fits in. Start by clicking "Arts & Humanities" on the main page (see Figure 14.8).

Figure 14.8
Categories on
Yahoo!'s main page.

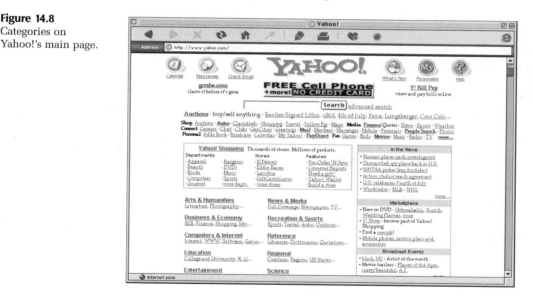

Then click "Crafts" to go the Crafts page (see Figure 14.9). You can then visit the categories listed here and determine which one works best for your site.

Figure 14.9
The Yahoo! Crafts
category leads to
more categories.

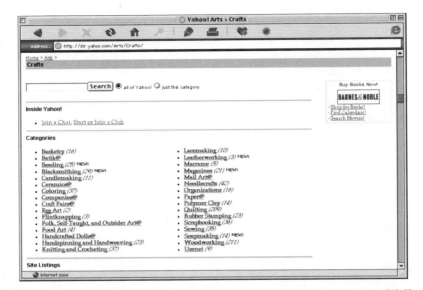

Once you have found your category, click "Suggest a Site" at the bottom of that page and follow the instructions (see Figure 14.10).

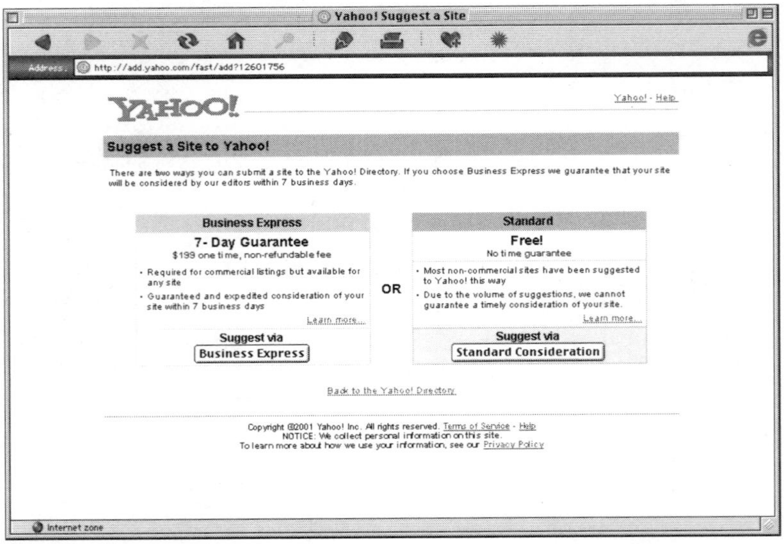

Figure 14.10
Yahoo! allows you to
make a submission in
one of two ways.

As you can see, you have two options. One is free; the other will guarantee only that your site will be considered promptly. This is not a guarantee that it will be listed.

E-mail and Discussion Lists

E-mail and discussion lists offer several opportunities for promoting your Web site, but you must always be aware of rules and etiquette.

E-mail

I want to begin this section by telling you what not to do. You may be familiar with the term "spam," which refers to unsolicited commercial e-mail. There are services out there that will offer to sell you huge mailing lists for you to use in sending advertisements. My advice is to just say no. Spamming is rude at best and illegal at worst, as some states have now passed laws against it.

There are ways to use e-mail in a positive manner. For example, always put the URL of your Web site in your e-mail signature. Also, you can use e-mail to send out a newsletter to your customers, and I'll get into that in more detail in a later section. Also, it's good to use e-mail for customer service. Always reply promptly to questions from visitors to your Web site

For tips on the dos and don'ts of e-mail, check out the E-Mail Etiquette page at **http://iwillfollow.com/email.htm** (see Figure 14.11).

Figure 14.11
E-mail Etiquette
offers tips on courteous
use of e-mail.

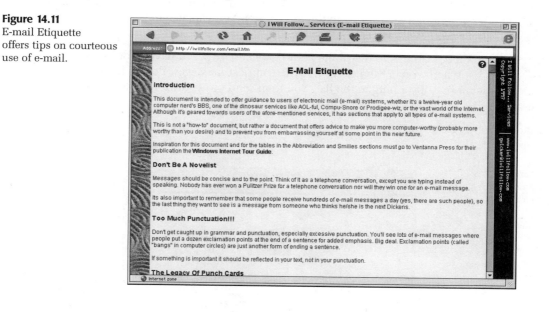

Discussion Lists

We talked a lot about discussion lists in Chapter 6. Just like e-mail, there are rules to be followed, but these rules vary from one list to another. For each mailing list you belong to, you should have received a list of rules when you first signed up. Go back and read them to gain an understanding of whether advertising is permitted and, if so, in what form.

Although advertising is usually frowned upon in discussion lists, it is usually acceptable to post a message when you are launching a brand-new Web site and invite people to visit. After that, simply include your URL in your signature so that it will show up every time you post a message to the list.

Even though you can't advertise outright, you can become known on a list by answering people's questions, giving tips, and otherwise engaging in constructive discussion. This increases your credibility, your visibility, and the visibility of your Web site. In addition to the URL in your signature, you can also include a one-line ad for a contest or a special offer.

If you think that a topic related to your Web site would be suitable for a discussion list, you can create your own discussion list and, therefore, your own rules. Yahoo! Groups provides the tools you need to create a discussion list, and there are other, similar services available.

Newsletters as a Marketing Tool

An e-mail newsletter can be an effective marketing tool, but in order to keep readers interested, you must include more than advertising.

First, let's look at how you get people to subscribe. You should never subscribe people to your newsletter without explicit instructions from them to do so. For people who order from you, you can offer an option to subscribe in the order form. You can also have a link on your home page enabling anyone who visits to subscribe.

You can use Yahoo! Groups to distribute your newsletter. All you have to do is create a discussion list where you are the only one who can post messages. People then subscribe to your newsletter by subscribing to the list. You then send out your newsletter by posting a message to the list.

Yahoo! Groups gives you a couple of ways to set up a subscription link on your site (see Figure 14.12).

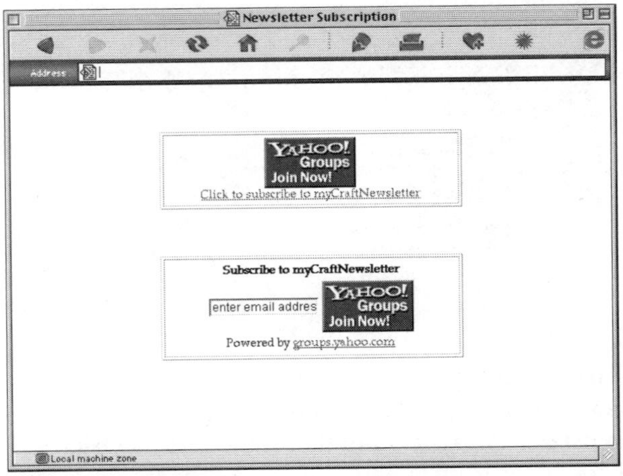

Figure 14.12
Yahoo! Groups makes it easy to subscribe with the click of your mouse.

If you decide to simply use e-mail to distribute your newsletter, you will need a mechanism on your Web site to collect the e-mail address of the subscribers (in other words, a form). Then you can use your e-mail program to send the newsletter. To maintain the privacy of your subscribers, you must put their e-mail addresses in the blind copy (Bcc) field of the message, so that the e-mail addresses will not be visible to the recipients.

As far as content is concerned, here are some ideas:

▶ What's new on the Web site

▶ One or two useful tips related to your craft

▶ A contest or promotion

▶ Specials

▶ How to unsubscribe

I suggest that you create your newsletter in plain text. Although most e-mail programs allow HTML formatting in messages, e-mail programs are somewhat inconsistent in how well they handle incoming mail that is formatted this way, so plain text is the safest way to go.

Finally, spell check and proofread your newsletter carefully, and don't forget to include a link back to your Web site.

Advertising

There are a lot of advertising opportunities on the Internet. In this section, we will look at various ways to use advertising to bring more visitors to your Web site. In choosing which method to use, you need to consider who are the people you want to reach and how much time and money you want to spend.

There is a tremendous amount of information available about online advertising. To get started, check out Promotion 101, at **http://www.promotion101.com/** (see Figure 14.13).

Figure 14.13
Promotion 101 can
teach you about
online advertising.

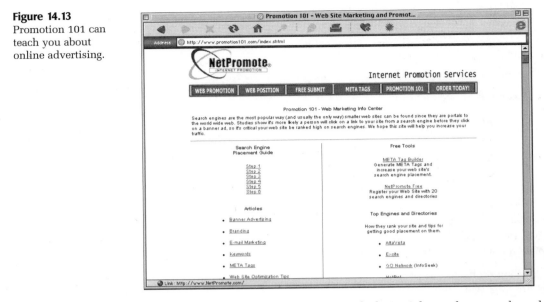

In addition to tips on search engine submissions, this site includes articles on banner ads and other types of advertising.

Banner Ads

If you have surfed the Web for more than a few minutes, you must certainly have encountered banner advertisements. Figure 14.14 shows an example of a banner ad on About.com.

Figure 14.14
A typical banner ad,
at the top of the page
and to the right of the
About logo.

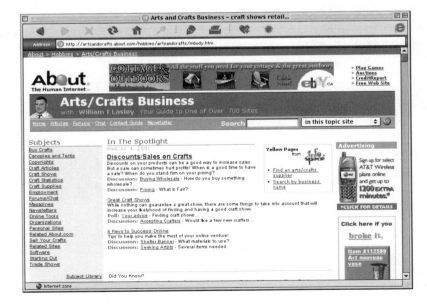

Ads like this appear on countless Web sites, and they are one of the methods available to you to advertise your site. As you might expect, the more prominent the site where you advertise, the more expensive the ad. Some of the more popular places to advertise are the big search engines and also About.com.

Designing a good banner ad can be a complex process. You need an ad that will attract people's attention without annoying them. The big advantage of banner ads is the visibility you get; the biggest disadvantage is the annoyance factor for the viewer. There are services you can hire to design banner ads for you, and there are also online tools like Animation.com's Banner Creator at **http://www.animation.com/** (see Figure 14.15).

Figure 14.15

Banner Creator provides online tools for building banner ads.

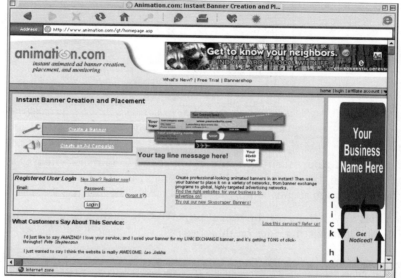

Section V Selling and Marketing Online

Now, let's look at how you pay for banner ads. First, though, a few definitions:

▶ The number of *impressions* is the number of times your ad is viewed.

▶ The *click-through ratio* is the number of people who clicked your ad divided by the number of people who saw it. For example, a click-through ratio of 2 percent means that two out of every one hundred people who saw your ad clicked it.

▶ Banner ads are usually charged for by *CPM*, or cost per thousand impressions (M is the Roman numeral for a thousand).

▶ Some hosts, such as **http://valueclick.com/**, charge for banners by CPC, or cost per click. You are charged only when your banner ad is clicked.

If you are going to pay for a banner ad, you want to target your audience as precisely as possible. For example, in search engines, it is possible to have your banner ad displayed when a certain keyword is entered in the search box.

For a lot more information and tips, check out the Banner Tips Web site at **http://bannertips.com/** (see Figure 14.16).

Figure 14.16
Banner Tips offers
information and advice.

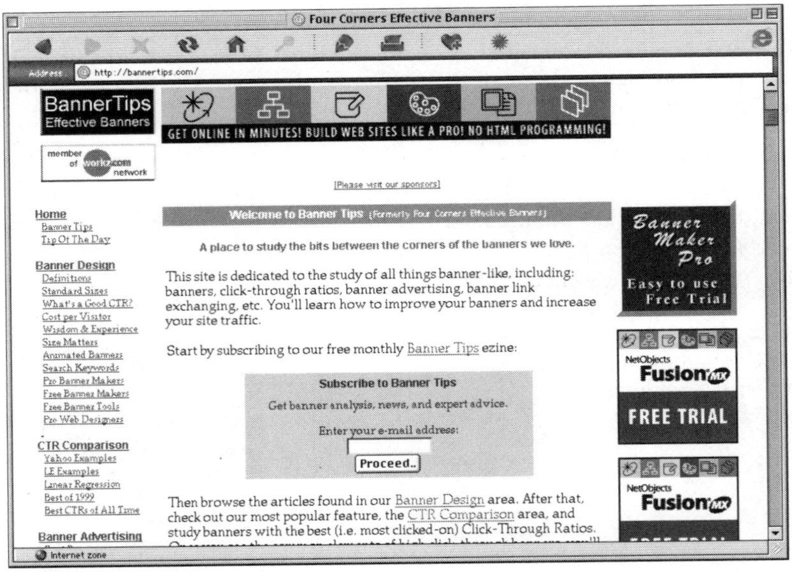

Web Rings

A Web ring is a group of sites on similar topics that are linked with a navigation bar that all members put on their home page. Using this navigation bar, visitors to one of the sites can jump to other sites in the ring by simply clicking a button. It's really a form of free banner exchange.

Yahoo! has a Web ring creation tool at **http://Webring.yahoo.com/** (see Figure 14.17). You can check out some existing rings on this site.

Figure 14.17
Yahoo! WebRing
helps you start, find,
or join a group of
related Web sites.

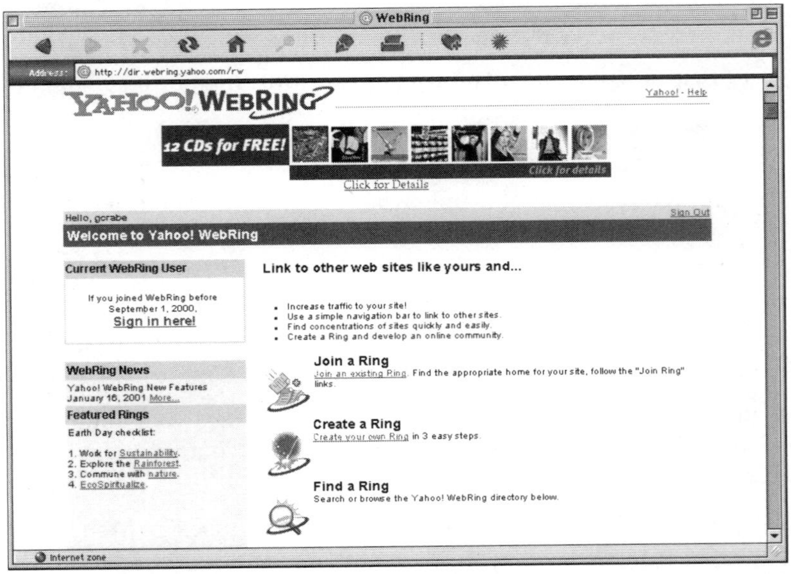

Web rings can have any number of members, from fewer than ten to several hundred. On the positive side, this can provide added traffic to your site. On the negative site, you have no control over the other sites in the ring. Some of them might be your competition, and some might no longer be there, causing broken links on your page, which doesn't leave a good impression with visitors.

More Advertising Opportunities

There are many inexpensive ways that you can advertise your Web site. For example, there are many electronic magazines out there, and you can become a sponsor, which means having your URL in every issue. Similarly, you can sponsor content on a Web site.

Charity events are always looking for items to give out as prizes in raffles during various events. Donate one of your craft items in exchange for an advertisement (including your URL) in the event program.

Promotion and Add-ons

There are a lot of ways to encourage repeat visits to your Web site. This section gives you a few examples. And remember to advertise all promotions in your e-mail newsletter.

Include your URL

Always include your Web site URL on everything:

- ▶ Business cards
- ▶ Letterhead
- ▶ Fax cover sheet
- ▶ Tags on your products
- ▶ E-mail signature
- ▶ Discussion list signature
- ▶ Brochures
- ▶ Anything else you hand out

Promotional Items

You can offer special promotional items on your Web site. In the previous chapter, for example, I mentioned CafePress.com as an easy way to offer T-shirts and other items with your own artwork.

There are also many Web sites where you can order personalized promotional items with your URL on them. One example is Kelly Specialties, at **http://www.adspecialties.net/** (see Figure 14.18).

Figure 14.18
Kelly Specialties is a Web site that sells personalized promotional items.

This site not only offers thousand of promotional items, but also promotion tips.

There are also promotional items you can make yourself with your computer, such as bookmarks, for example. You can create an image with your logo or a picture of one of your crafted items, include your e-mail address and your URL, and print it out on card stock.

Special Promotions

Here are a few other things you can do to keep people coming back to your Web site:

▶ Offer something for free, perhaps a downloadable pattern of one of your designs.

▶ Offer discounts for repeat customers.

▶ Sponsor contests.

▶ Run a Pattern of the Month club (or replace "pattern" with something else you sell). This means that people will sign up in advance for twelve purchases.

Web Site Awards and Other Listings

There are a huge number of Web site awards available out there, some more meaningful than others. The Website Awards Web site, at **http://Websiteawards.xe.net/** (see Figure 14.19), helps to sort it all out for you.

Figure 14.19
Website Awards brings together award sites from all over the Web.

This Web site lists many places you can submit your site for awards. Another place you could submit your site to is the Yahoo! Picks of the Week at **http://www.yahoo.com/picks/**. This is a weekly e-mail with wide readership.

Links

Another feature you can add to your Web site is a page of links to resources that are related to the topic of your site. One drawback of this feature is that you have to constantly check to make sure these links are still good.

There is an online tool that can help you with this. For a small fee, NetMechanic, at **http://www.netmechanic.com/** (see Figure 14.20), will check your site for broken links. It offers a lot of other services as well.

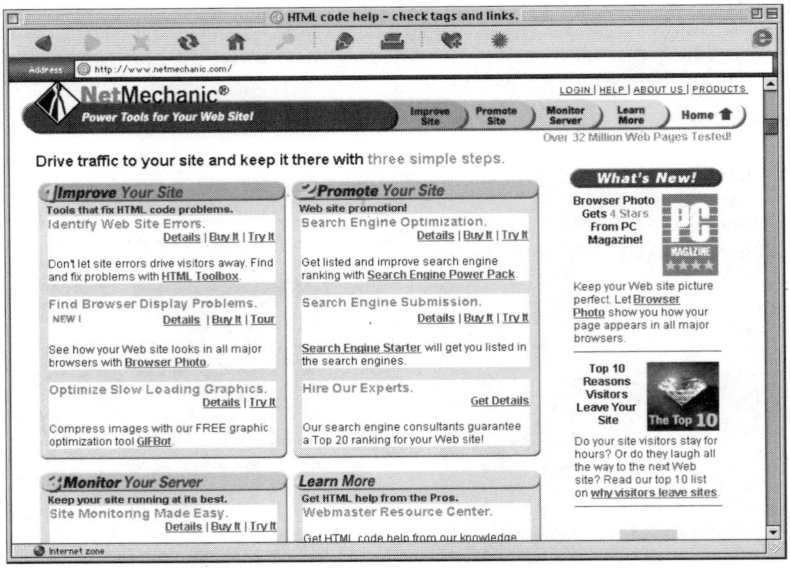

Figure 14.20
NetMechanic can help you check for broken links.

Another good site, Web Site Garage, at **http://www.Websitegarage.com/,** offers similar services.

You can also offer reciprocal links to other Web sites that represent related businesses. This means that you will put in a link to their Web site if they put in a link to yours.

Measuring Success

There are several ways to measure the success of your Web site. First, if you are selling something, you know how many orders you are getting. You can request feedback from visitors by having them fill out a form. You can also create an online survey, as described in Chapter 13.

To measure the popularity of your Web site, your hosting service should be able to provide regular statistics on the number of visitors to your site, which pages are the most viewed, and so on.

Link popularity—how many other sites have links to your site—is another important measure, since it can influence your ranking in a search engine. Go to the Link Popularity Web site at **http://www.linkpopularity.com/** to check the popularity of your site.

Going Forward

This chapter has just scratched the surface when it comes to marketing your Web site. I want to leave you with some good resource sites for more information on this topic.

TIP

If you want to expand your knowledge in this area, I recommend this book: *101 Ways to Promote Your Web Site* by Susan Sweeney (Maximum Press, 2001, ISBN 1885068573).

Cre8pc Website Promotion, at **http://www.cre8pc.com/** (see Figure 14.21) offers not only information on optimizing your site for search engines, but also useful tips on user-interface design and usability.

Figure 14.21
Cre8pc: Website Promotion and user-interface design information.

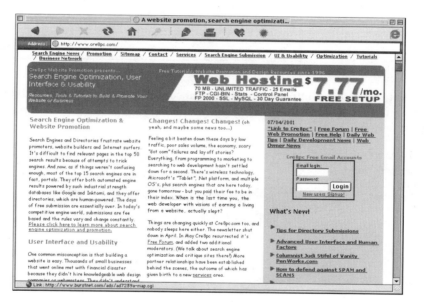

Adbility, at **http://adbility.com/** (see Figure 14.22) contains a large collection of links to affiliate programs, search engine information, banner ad creation services, and more.

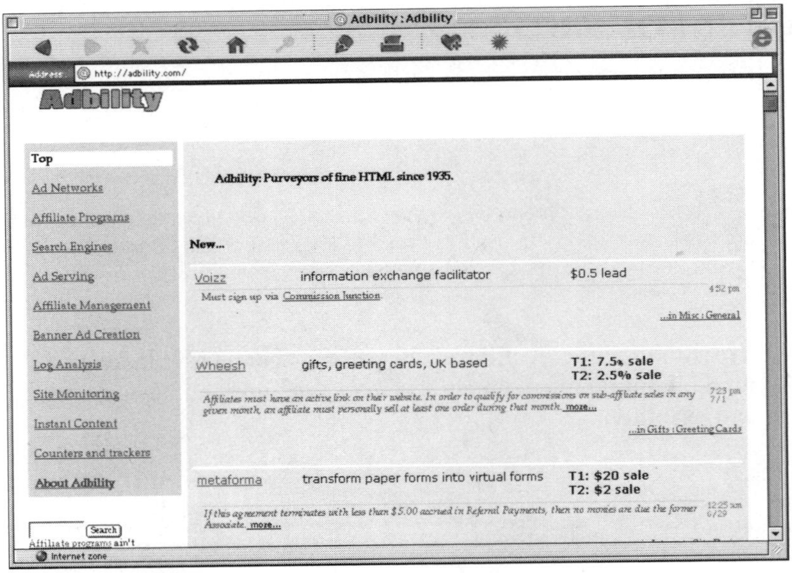

Figure 14.22
Adbility: A collection
of links to advertising
opportunities.

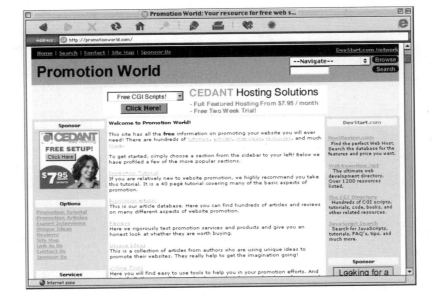

Promotion World, at **http://promotionworld.com/** (see Figure 14.23), contains not only links and
resources, but also free information on promoting your Web site including tutorials, articles, and
interviews.

Figure 14.23
Promotion World:
Tutorials, articles,
and reviews.

Index

Index

crafters'
Internet Handbook

Research, Connect and Sell
Your Crafts Online

Geneviève Crabe

Crafters' Internet Handbook

All copyrights and trademarks used as examples or references in this book are retained by their individual owners, including the following:

Caricature on back cover created by Dennis Porter (www.drawme.com)

"The Creative Internet" (Chapter 4) and "The Memory Box Program," by Tera Leigh (Chapter 8)

"Why Care About Copyrights in Crafts?" by Susan Brandt (Chapter 5)

Interview with Anne Strebe (Chapter 6)

Interview with Heather Fox (Chapter 7)

Shelley McCoy (quote in Chapter 8)

Beth Koskie (quote in Chapter 8)

Interview with Phyllis Tilford (Chapter 12)

Sharon Saunders (quote in "Final Words")

Credits: Cover and interior design, Michelle Frey, Stephanie Japs, Cathie Tibbetts, Kevin Vollrath, and John Windhorst, DOV Graphics; development editor, Sherri Osborn; senior editor, Mark Garvey; publishing assistant, Rodney Wilson.

Publisher: Andy Shafran

Library of Congress Catalog Number 2001086927

ISBN 1-929685-43-2

5 4 3 2 1

Educational facilities, companies, and organizations interested in multiple copies or licensing of this book should contact the publisher for quantity discount information. Training manuals, CD-ROMs, and portions of this book are also available individually or can be tailored for specific needs.

MUSKA&LIPMAN

Muska & Lipman Publishing
2645 Erie Avenue, Suite 41
Cincinnati, Ohio 45208
www.muskalipman.com
publisher@muskalipman.com